"DuBois shows a keen knowledge of river running and has done exhaustive research in putting his work together. It is rare that you have such a fine author and an excellent whitewater man, all in one."

—Don Hatch, Don Hatch River
Expeditions

"Despite the [river's] changes, DuBois' nostalgic return connects the exploratory spirit of his pioneering voyage with the celebrations of today's whitewater experience."

—George Thomas, Editor
CANOE

"DuBois reminds of the past, and subtly cautions us on the effects of the popularity of the sport. Make no mistake, this book is history—a history of something lost, and, hopefully, a lesson of something to be gained for all boaters in the future."

—Ken Hulick, Editor
RIVER RUNNER

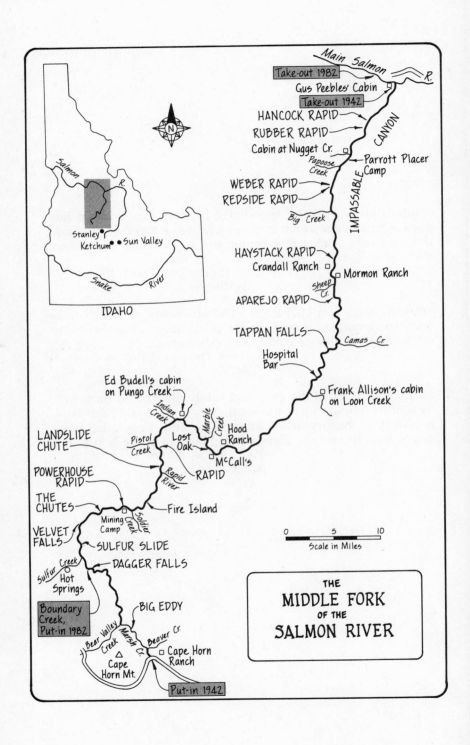

Main Salmon R.

Take-out 1982
Gus Peebles' Cabin
Take-out 1942
HANCOCK RAPID
RUBBER RAPID
Cabin at Nugget Cr.
Papoose Creek
Parrott Placer Camp
WEBER RAPID
REDSIDE RAPID
Big Creek

IMPASSABLE CANYON

HAYSTACK RAPID
Crandall Ranch
Mormon Ranch
Sheep Cr.
APAREJO RAPID

TAPPAN FALLS
Camas Cr.
Hospital Bar

Ed Budell's cabin on Pungo Creek
Frank Allison's cabin on Loon Creek
Indian Creek
Marble Creek
LANDSLIDE CHUTE
Pistol Creek
Lost Oak
Hood Ranch
POWERHOUSE RAPID
Rapid River
McCall's
RAPID
THE CHUTES
Mining Camp
Soldier Creek
Fire Island
VELVET FALLS
SULFUR SLIDE
DAGGER FALLS
Sulfur Creek
Hot Springs
Boundary Creek, Put-in 1982
BIG EDDY
Bear Valley Creek
Marsh Cr.
Beaver Cr.
Cape Horn Ranch
Cape Horn Mt.
Put-in 1942

Salmon R.
Stanley
Ketchum • Sun Valley
Snake River
IDAHO

N

0   5   10
Scale in Miles

THE
MIDDLE FORK
OF THE
SALMON RIVER

Eliot DuBois

AN
INNOCENT
ON THE
MIDDLE FORK

A Whitewater Adventure
in
Idaho's Wilderness

Drawings by Betsy James

THE MOUNTAINEERS

Seattle

THE MOUNTAINEERS: Organized 1906
". . . to explore, preserve and enjoy
the natural beauty of the Northwest."

Published by The Mountaineers
306 Second Avenue West, Seattle, Washington 98119

Published simultaneously in Canada by
Douglas & McIntyre Ltd.
1615 Venables Street, Vancouver, B.C. V5L 2H1

Manufactured in the United States of America
Copyedited by Barbara Chasan
Cover design by Elizabeth Watson
Map by Newell Cartographics

Cover photos:

Background—One of the quiet stretches of the Middle Fork, about a mile below
Marble Creek, August, 1982. (Photo by Eliot DuBois)

Inset—The author as he departed from Marsh Creek, 1942. The photo was
taken by Slim Hendrick, at whose ranch DuBois stayed before beginning his
solo descent of the Middle Fork. DuBois received this photo in 1982, following
his second river journey, from Hendrick's widow, Mildred.

Library of Congress Cataloging-in-Publication Data

DuBois, Eliot.
    An innocent on the Middle Fork.

    1. Kayak touring--Idaho--Salmon River, Middle Fork.
2. Rafting (Sports)--Idaho--Salmon River, Middle Fork.
3. Salmon River, Middle Fork (Idaho)--Description and
travel.   I. Title.
GV776.I22S253   1987   917.96'78   86-31088
ISBN 0-89886-125-X

0 9 8 7
5 4 3 2 1

Foreword

Excitement, reflection, change: these are river themes. And these are the themes of Eliot DuBois' *An Innocent on the Middle Fork,* one of the most literate and engaging books I have ever come across with the river as protagonist. It is profound and fun.

The book is a richly textured tale of two boat trips—forty years apart—down Idaho's Middle Fork of the Salmon River. The first trip took place in 1942, when the world was at war. DuBois, then twenty years old, celebrated his last summer before entering the service with a reckless solo kayak trip down a river that was then as remote and little known as those of New Guinea are today. DuBois' voyage took place before there were fiberglass hulls, wetsuits, and eskimo rolls; before river running had become so popular that federal regulation of the sport became necessary along the Middle Fork in order to save the river from those who would love it to death.

An Innocent on the Middle Fork reads like an account of a modern-day exploratory river expedition, with the reader breathlessly anticipating the view and obstacles around each turn in the canyon. The author's detailed observations of people, places, and events along the river are extraordinary—as fresh as morning news and more engaging. Yet the young DuBois' keen eye surpasses his juvenile judgment. He runs rapids without scouting, forgets his life jacket at one point, and breaks his own cardinal rule of later years by boating alone.

The heart of the book is this first journey, a classic rite of passage, complete with tests of skill and cunning, unforeseen obstacles, great danger and final enlightenment. It's hair-raising, shirt-soaking adventure—and a celebration. But the soul is DuBois' second trip forty years later, when he measures the river's changes as though they were his own. He regrets that regulations now control everything from fire building to toilet procedures on the Middle Fork but marvels that the rapids, walls, and rocks remain so unchanged, and that the values of the wilderness experience endure.

I, too, experienced the wealth and wrath of the Middle Fork when, in 1971, I attempted the run in a clumsy, half-rotted, thin-skinned inflatable called a basketboat. I ripped out the bottom in Velvet Falls, broke the frame in Pistol Creek, and spent a week limping downstream. The river pummeled me, but allowed me through its gates intact, scarred but stronger, healthy but humbled. I sang at the take-out.

The Middle Fork is a grand river, and Eliot DuBois is an eloquent guide through its wild waters and the rapids of change.

Richard Bangs, President,
Sobek Expeditions;
Co-author of *River Gods*

Contents

Acknowledgments

Memories, plus an almost forgotten file of old letters, telegrams, notes, and maps were the first references for the writing of this book. Many people assisted in its completion. Correspondence with Ed Friedman, Mildred Hendrick, and Ed Budell stimulated the process of recall. Specific information and suggestions, as well as general encouragement, came from river runners including Ken Horwitz, Bob McNair, John Bryant, and Don Hatch and his son Barry. I am indebted to Hugh M. "Mac" Thompson and to Ted Anderson of the Forest Service. Both were more than generous with their time in interview and correspondence. Cort Conley supplied information concerning the hermit Earl Parrott. In addition, much of the history of the river was derived from the excellent book which Conley co-authored with Johnney Carrey (*The Middle Fork and the Sheepeater War*. Cambridge, Idaho: Backeddy Books, 1980). For companionship and forbearance on the river, my thanks to Francisco Guevara, Mark Franklin, Marjorie Wood, Rene Zamora, Dottie Shelton, Eric and Jayne Plicard. For editorial tolerance, high marks to Donna DeShazo, Steve Whitney, Ann Cleeland, and Barbara Chasan. Thanks also to illustrator Betsy James.

My family has been supportive in many ways. I am glad that my mother, the late Theodora DuBois, a prolific writer, lived to learn of the acceptance of her son's first book. I was encouraged by my sister Dora, a foldboater in the early days, and by my two sons, river runners both, Cornelius "Kin," and Delafield

"Del." I thank Del for organizing and leading the 1982 trip. Finally, I owe more than I can express to the patience, the encouraging attitude, and the critical instinct of my wife Barbara, with whom I have shared so much of the magic of whitewater.

AN
INNOCENT
ON THE
MIDDLE FORK

Boundary Creek launch site for the Middle Fork, August 19, 1982

August 19, 1982

Point of Entry

Barbara and I stood on the edge of the bank and peered down to where, some sixty feet below, the river swept from right to left then out of sight into First Bend Rapid.

"It looks low," Barbara said.

"It is," I answered. "The sign on the office says 2.74; that's this morning's gauge reading."

"So, what does that mean?"

"It's more water than when Del ran it in '78 but much less than when I ran it in '42. The upper river will be a bit shallow, but we'll get through."

As we watched, a McKenzie drift boat, a high-sided dorytype rowboat, detached itself from the bank. There were two people in the boat, an oarsman and a passenger. The water was so transparent that from this angle the boat appeared to float in midair above the perfectly visible granite boulders of the river bottom. The oarsman took a stroke so as to face downstream, and the dimple left by his oar defined the surface of the water, breaking the illusion. Guided by a few oar strokes, the boat threaded its way between some small rocks that broke the surface at the beginning of the rapid, accelerated in faster water, and disappeared around the bend.

On the rocky beach below us there was one more McKenzie boat, a dozen rafts, and several inflatable kayaks. The sound of excited voices drifted up to us. People were tying in their supplies and equipment, getting ready to shove off. To our right several young Forest Service employes were horsing a big sweep raft from a trailer onto the wooden ramp that led from the staging area down to the water. Two members of our party, Cisco and Mark, helped them. To our left was a small building with the sign "Office" above the door. From inside came the cackle of a short-wave radio, the voice of Ted Anderson, River Manager, fifty miles away at headquarters in Challis.

In spite of the office, the radio, the ramp, and the bustle of boaters getting ready, there was still some wilderness in this setting. Above us and feathered by timber except on the steepest places, the canyon walls sloped up to meet a sky that was as clear as the river below. To the east, over the top of the canyon we could see a cloud. The weather, bright sunshine, cool clear air but with a hint at an afternoon storm, matched our feelings: joy at the prospect of being on a river once again but, mixed with that, a gut-tightening anxiety that would be with us until we were on the rafts and under way.

We were at Boundary Creek, the official launch site for Idaho's Middle Fork of the Salmon River, one of America's most popular whitewater rivers. We were about to begin an eight-day, one-hundred-mile raft trip down challenging rapids and through spectacular canyons. The year was 1982, but the conditions that we encountered were typical of any year since river usage was stabilized. Eight thousand people run the

Middle Fork every year, the majority as passengers on commercial trips operated by licensed outfitters. Ours was a private trip, and the trip leader was our younger son Del. The other members of the party were friends of Del's, most of them veterans of many river-running adventures. Barbara and I were to ride as passengers in Del's raft, but we too have a whitewater background, though our days of canoeing and kayaking are long past. We relate to a period before the rivers became crowded with boaters and before the mass invasion of the American Wilderness. In our time, a put-in place was not a well-designed facility but only a spot where road and river casually came together, and where it just happened to be possible to slither down the bank with canoes and kayaks. We relate to a period before rivers were managed and controlled.

On this trip, we discovered an astonishing degree of control. The most serious obstacle was not any one of the seven Class IV rapids that waited for us downstream nor any one of the hundreds of lesser rapids. We'd already passed the most serious obstacle, which was getting approval to run the river and a starting date from the Forest Service. Del had applied the past winter, but so many boaters wanted to run this river that our chances had been one in five. The Middle Fork is not one of the most difficult rivers by modern standards, but it has an important place in the repertoire of whitewater rivers. We were lucky; we received a starting date, though it was August 19, our third choice, later in the season than we'd hoped, and therefore at low stage of water. No matter, we had survived the bureaucratic rapid and were ready to take on the real rapids.

I had challenged the rapids of the Middle Fork once before. That was forty years earlier, when no more than five or six people ran the river each year. At that time there was no road to Boundary Creek, and I had passed this spot at the beginning of my third day.

My reasons for coming back were several: There was the usual need for a vacation, the need for a clean break from the stresses of everyday modern life. Beyond that, I wanted to show Barbara the river that I sometimes think of as my own, not too illogical a thought because the river flows through National Forest land, has been designated by Congress a Wild and Scenic River, and so is a part of my property. I was here to see how my river had fared in the intervening forty years. I wanted to see to what extent the features of the river and the canyon had changed. I wanted to see what had happened to the frontier environment that made such an impression on me in 1942. I wanted to determine if it were still possible to have a personally significant wilderness experience by running the river, or whether the only possible experience was a variety of amusement park ride. I wanted to form an opinion as to whether the Forest Service was doing a creditable job of managing the river. Were they adequately serving the general public, the dedicated river runners, and the river itself? What of the whole concept of river-use management? Was it necessary and did it work?

I'd already taken steps to find answers to these questions. Two days earlier, Barbara and I had been in Challis, Idaho. I visited the Forest Service offices there and had a talk with Mac Thompson, Middle Fork District Ranger, and with Ted Anderson, River Manager. These gentlemen were most generous with their time. Perhaps it helps to be a white-haired survivor of an earlier age. We discussed the problems of allotting starting dates to the professional outfitters and to the ever-increasing ranks of private boaters. I had come away from the interview with a better appreciation of the problem and a feeling that Mac and Ted were competent and well-intentioned men, doing their best in a difficult situation. Now I would see how well these intentions translate into practice. But I had not come to the river so much to check on these particular people or even on the Forest Service as to check on how the modern world was treating its wilderness. Not too well, I suspected.

The Forest Service boat was now in the water. Barbara and I

helped carry one of our rafts to the ramp. It was a heavy and awkward load. Mark tied a rope to the rear of the raft, looped the rope over a timber of the ramp structure, and belayed the raft as it slid down into the water. We carried waterproof duffle bags and boxes of supplies down a trail on the far side of the office. Del tied them into his raft, securing the load with a cargo net. Everything was ready, but there was one more ritual to go through before we left.

We gathered near the office building for a briefing by a freckle-faced girl in a Forest Service uniform. She was Penny Brown, a Student Conservation Association intern, earning college credits as she spent the summer working for the Forest Service. Penny instructed us in the rules for camping during our trip. The object of these rules was to insure minimum human impact on the canyon. Some of these rules were new to Barbara and me, but they were quite familiar to Del and his friends. For instance, all boating parties had to carry a metal pan in which to build fires. The procedure was to set the pan on rocks so as not to scorch the ground. Ashes, trash, and all human waste, unless campgrounds had privies, had to be contained and carried by the boating party to a disposal location at the end of the trip.

When Penny had finished her talk, she asked if there were any questions. Mark asked about wildlife. Following a big fire in 1979, a wolf was sighted. Had any more been seen? Penny had nothing to report on wolves but said that we might see bighorn sheep in the Impassable Canyon. Penny wished us a good trip and then asked each of us to sign a statement certifying that ours was a private trip with expenses shared equally by all members. Del, as trip leader, had more documents to sign. When this was done, we hurried down the trail to where the rafts were tied up. I had a feeling that this place and the process we'd been through were more appropriate to a rocket launching to the moon than to the beginning of a river trip.

There were ten of us in four rafts. Jayne and Eric, both

intensive-care nurses and therefore a valuable asset on any such trip, were in one raft. Mark, a serious young man with an encyclopedic knowledge of the wilderness, commanded the smallest raft. His passenger was Rene, a young man seldom without either a spinning rod or a beer can in hand. Mardi, a skier and horseback rider from Colorado, and Dottie, youngest of the group, fragile looking, with a mop of curly blond hair, rode with Cisco. Cisco, resembling a Spanish nobleman in a painting by Velásquez or perhaps a pirate, except that he wore an enormous black cowboy hat that he had won at a two-step dance contest, manned the oars of the largest raft, named the Francesca. Barbara and I rode with Del, a rugged and competent thirty-year-old with extensive experience on rivers, on mountains, and in the desert.

We climbed aboard in the approved way, sitting on the side of the raft and sloshing our feet in the water so as not to track sand or gravel into the raft, then swinging our feet up and in. Barbara and I occupied the front of the raft. Our responsibilities, besides hanging on, were to bail and to keep track of where we were. For this we used a booklet published by the Forest Service. It contained excellent maps of the river as well as brief descriptions of the major rapids. When we were ready, Del shoved the boat away from the bank and climbed aboard. He took his place amidships at the oars, facing downstream, looking over our heads. Behind him were a mound of waterproof duffle bags and a big cooler full of food. Fishing rods and cameras were available. Everything was tied down. We were under way.

It had been so long since we'd been on a river that the sensation was at first very strange, as though the raft were stationary and the river were moving past us. We slipped between rocks and through First Bend Rapid. None of it looked familiar, but would I remember much after forty years? Because of the low water, it was not easy to pick a course. Del was in command of the raft, but he was open to suggestion. Our voices were elevated above the sound of the rapids.

"Over there, near the right bank, there seems to be water."

"But look out for the black rock."

"I see it."

In a little over a mile, we slid through a series of sharp bends, and there on the left a tributary creek came in.

"That's Sulfur Creek," I shouted. "It's just as I remember it. I crossed over here and landed just below where the creek comes in."

We drifted on. I scanned the left bank for a spot that had stuck in my memory. I found it.

"Right up there on the bank I saw a badger."

I had made the connection from 1982 back to 1942, and as we went down the river, one raft among many rafts, almost a parade of rafts, I also saw myself, a lonely kayaker on a deserted river. In particular, I made the connection at the big rapids, places where I had experienced some crisis or some element of fear. The rapids formed by landslide had been drastically changed by erosion, but enough of the surrounding topography remained so that I could picture them as they had been. The drops formed by resistant rock ledges appeared to have changed not at all, and I was able to identify exactly where I had taken my kayak over a drop or through a narrow slot between rock walls. My most haunting perception was at the long rapid called Powerhouse. In the upper portion of the rapid, entering the turn to the right, I pointed out to Barbara and Del where I had swung into an eddy and landed below the old mining camp. The river was dropping steeply at this point and Del commented, "You must have been getting good." Then as we rounded the bend and threaded our way through the lower half of Powerhouse, I looked up at the low cliff on the right and saw myself, peering down at the rapid, scouting my course. At the bottom of Powerhouse, where the river charged info the cliff, I looked to the left and pictured where I had taken my kayak out of harm's way over a submerged gravel bar that at this much lower stage of water was high and dry.

That evening, at our campfire, Del's friends asked questions about my early trip. I tried to explain as best I could. Next morning, when three young Forest Service employes, taking their sweep raft down the river, stopped to check out our campsite, they too were interested. I was a link to the river's history. I found it easy to talk about the physical aspects of the river, what had changed and what hadn't. It was also relatively easy to describe my equipment and to contrast it with modern equipment. What was difficult was to convey what it was like to live in the world of 1942 and to belong to that very small group of people who had limited equipment and skill but who undertook to run difficult and dangerous rivers. It was equally difficult to convey something of the life of the people who lived as a scattered frontier community along the banks of this river. It was more difficult to explain what drove me, in violation of all modern whitewater safety rules and in violation of common sense at any period, to run this river alone. It was most difficult to explain the effect that passage down the river and through the canyons had on me. This would take more than answering a few questions around a campfire.

1

Whitewater Dreams

When I first experienced whitewater, at age fifteen, I knew that as much as I wanted to do anything, I wanted to run rivers. The sound of rapids ahead, the tug of water on the hull of the canoe, the filaments of current curling around rocks, the heaping up of waves, all produced a mind set that would lead to an inevitable contest. Somewhere a river waited for me, and that river would put me to the test and be the losing of my innocence. Not that my history is unique. The running of rivers ranges from the benign to the dangerous. The wise and reasonable approach is to start at the easy end of the spectrum and to move gradually toward greater challenges, approaching some limit imposed by skill and temperament. Yet there is an interaction between the boater and river that can confound wisdom and reason, moving the process too fast and too far. The story of how I came to run the Middle Fork is an example.

In 1937 and again in 1938 I went on month-long canoe trips in northern Maine. In heavily laden twenty-foot canoes we toiled up and down windblown lakes, then descended the Allegash and the St. John rivers to the Canadian border. I learned much on those trips but lacked the strength and coordination to be given what I most wanted, which was to be put in charge of a canoe in rapids.

At that time my family lived in a Connecticut town through which flowed a small river, the Shepaug. I had fished this river, and I recognized that it had rapids much like those I had experienced in Maine. In those days, shooting the rapids was an integral part of north-woods travel; it was seldom thought of as a sport in itself. But here was a perfectly good river. Why not run it? For thirty dollars, the standard price for a good used canoe, I bought a sixteen-foot Oldtown. Its construction was canvas on wood, and its hull shape was better suited to a quiet evening's paddle on a lake than to running whitewater, but still it was a canoe. I recruited bow paddlers: school companions, various girlfriends, my sister, anyone foolish enough to get into the boat with me. I started with the easiest section of the river, and when I could run that without upsetting, moved on to the next more difficult, moving on again until I had run the whole river. I ran the Shepaug in every water condition and season, when the water was high and full of floating ice to when there was barely a trickle to float the canoe and cool the hot stones of the riverbed. I came to know each heron and kingfisher along the bank. I knew the river at all times of day. I even ran one section by moonlight.

In the same time period, I made contact with a group of young men and women from New York City who had similar interests. They had formed a club, at first to ski. But as the snow on the ski slopes melted and ran down into the valleys, these skiers gravitated toward river running, finding a way to extend the season. They also found it pleasant to sit on a river-bank when the sun was shining and the trees were beginning to leaf out. From time to time, my sister and I joined this group, first on the Shepaug, then on the Ten Mile and the Housatonic.

Instead of using canoes, this group used foldboats, a German-developed folding kayak. Foldboats were very popular in Europe, where most people relied on public transportation. A couple living in an apartment could store a boat in the closet, take it by train to the bank of a river, run downstream, stop at inns or hostels for the night, and finally return home by train. In the twenties and thirties, foldboats were brought back to the United States by people who had used them during vacations in Europe. There was also one American manufacturer. The design was ingenious. To assemble, a wood frame was slipped inside a rubberized canvas hull and then forced outward until the boat was quite rigid. The hull was strong enough to resist minor abrasions. Punctures could be fixed with inner-tube patching material.

These boats were longer and broader of beam than modern whitewater kayaks. The keel was straight when viewed from the side, making the boats hard to turn. Cockpit openings were large. A big wave sloshing over the cockpit coaming was likely to collapse the flimsy spray cover that snapped around the boater's waist, with the frequent result of a swamped boat and a cold swim in the river.

Dunkings were common among my foldboating friends, most of whom had a slap-dash approach to whitewater. A few were more skilled, in particular the man who was to become my link to the Middle Fork. That man was Alexander "Zee" Grant. His technique was to choose his course through rapids very carefully and then to maneuver among rocks and waves with just a few guiding strokes. There was much to be learned from watching Zee handle whitewater.

Zee worked as a publicist for the Union Pacific Railroad. His job was to promote U. P.'s new Idaho resort, Sun Valley. This assignment gave him almost unlimited free train travel and the opportunity to expand his whitewater horizons.

At that time, western rivers were the province of a few professional boaters who used various types of rowboats and scows. The Grand Canyon of the Colorado was a famous whitewater run but was attempted so infrequently that each trip was called an expedition. In Oregon there was a well-established tradition of whitewater boating. Guides took fishermen down the Rogue, McKenzie, and other rivers. Their boat was the McKenzie drift boat. In Idaho, on the Main Salmon, large scows, up to forty feet long, carried equipment and supplies to mining camps along the river. Zee felt that the big western rivers could also be run by amateur boaters using foldboats, a low-cost approach to wilderness adventure. His object was not just to run the rivers but to write articles, give lectures, and generally to promote whitewater boating.

In 1938 he ran an upper portion of the Main Salmon from the town of Stanley down through Shotgun Rapid, a formidable drop that had received its name when two men swamped their canoe and lost a valuable shotgun. The following year, Zee teamed up with W. Stewart Gardiner of Salt Lake City to run Lodore, Whirlpool, and Split Mountain canyons of the Green River, all within Dinosaur National Monument and to this day a classic whitewater run.

Zee's next target was the Middle Fork of the Salmon, a river that had seldom been run and that had the reputation of being one of the toughest in the West. In the 1920s a veteran Main Salmon scow pilot named Captain Harry Guleke bypassed the upper reaches by packing in to the river. He built a log raft and floated the lower canyons. In the same decade, a party of canoeists ran the entire river from Bear Valley Creek to the confluence with the Main Salmon. Low water and a passage time of several months made their trip possible but none the less remarkable. In 1936 a party of river runners from Utah using compartmented rowboats ran the Middle Fork and continued on down the Main Salmon to Riggins. The leaders of that trip were

Bus Hatch, Frank Swain, and Dr. Russell G. Frazier. Frazier and Swain led a return trip in 1939, the same year that an Oregon guide named Woodie Hindman and his wife Ruth ran the river in a McKenzie drift boat. Woodie Hindman and three other guides were back in 1940, the year that Zee made his run.

Zee arrived on the banks of Bear Valley Creek on August 11. He had two companions, Rodney Aller, a competent fold-boater, and Coleman Nimick, who had no previous whitewater experience. The water was very low, exposing rocks and limiting the choice of channel. Zee and Aller, for all their experience, had their hands full. Nimick, as might be expected, had a great deal of trouble. Still, when they reached Gus Peebles's cabin at the confluence with the Main Salmon, on August 22, they could look back on a thrilling adventure.

I did not cross paths with Zee and didn't hear him describe his Middle Fork trip until the Fourth of July weekend of 1941, when about fifty river runners gathered at Middledam, Maine, for the Second Annual National Whitewater Championships. In 1941, fifty river runners constituted a large percentage of the whitewater enthusiasts in the northeastern states. Races were held on the Rapid River, a steep and narrow stream that runs between two lakes of the Rangely Chain. It was indicative of the beginning stages of whitewater boating that most of those participating wound up with swamped or smashed boats. I entered the "Open Race," so called because anyone could enter in any form of boat. The name was also well-deserved because the race organizers opened the sluice gates of the dam at the head of the river. I used a boat that I had designed and built myself, a cross between a foldboat and a canoe, and I succeeded in finishing still afloat. My time earned me second place. This inflated my ego. Equally important for this story, the experience of sliding down steep inclines of water past rumbling foam-filled holes and of smashing through waves that broke over my head impressed on me that the Shepaug and the Housatonic would no longer do. I must seek bigger water, tougher rivers.

I talked with Zee. He suggested that I join him on a Grand

Canyon trip that he was planning for later that same summer. The Grand Canyon had never been successfully run by a paddle-propelled boat. Zee, with characteristic optimism, felt that he could do it. His plan was to go through the canyon in company with Norman Nevills, a professional who took passengers down the Colorado in big, compartmented rowboats. Zee wanted a second foldboater to go along and had asked Jack Kissner of Folbot Corporation to make two oversized foldboats. Although I had been puffed up by my performance in the Open Race, I recalled John Wesley Powell's lurid account of his 1869 expedition through the canyons of the Colorado. I suspected that I wasn't yet ready for that challenge. Equally important, I didn't have enough money. I had a good job that summer, making all of twenty dollars a week, and had hopes of saving enough to finance a river trip the following summer, but 1941 was out. I regretfully declined Zee's offer but, with 1942 in mind, asked him if he thought I could handle the Middle Fork.

"If you can run the Rapid River, you can run the Middle Fork," said Zee. "The upper section is something like the Rapid River. They're both steep and rocky. Then the Middle Fork gets much bigger."

"As big as the Housatonic?" I asked.

"Bigger," said Zee. "The Middle Fork is a small river to begin with, but quite steep. It picks up water from side creeks so that it's constantly growing larger. The middle section of the river is relatively easy, except for a few spots; then the river gets very tough again. It goes through a steep-sided canyon called the Impassable Canyon. The rapids in that section are powerful. They tend to be short and steep, with calmer water between, like giant steps."

"What about the fishing?" I asked.

"The fishing is fantastic."

I knew then that I would have to go to Idaho to experience for myself the canyons, the rapids, the fishing. The next year, 1942, would be my year to run the Middle Fork.

In September, I began my junior year at Yale. In spite of studies and other interests, the running of the Middle Fork remained a major goal and preoccupation. It was not easy to translate the dream into a reality. There were problems of finding companions for the trip, problems of equipment, training, transportation. Information was a problem. At the mammoth Sterling Memorial Library, the only reference to the Middle Fork that I could find was a geological map that showed that in its upper reaches and again in its lowest section, the river had cut down into a granite formation. The middle section ran through metamorphic rock. That accounted for the tough upper section, the easier middle, and the formidable final section.

In November I went to a meeting of whitewater boaters. The official purpose of the meeting was to form a nationwide organization to be called River Rats of America. This was Zee's idea. The concept was greeted with enthusiasm, but no action was taken because everyone present believed that we would soon be at war. River Rats would have to wait. In spite of the shadow of the war, the meeting was enjoyable. We watched movies, the most spectacular of which were Zee's films of his Grand Canyon run. The water was high and the boats were often lost from view among the waves. Zee's feat of kayaking the Grand Canyon was not repeated for nineteen years. He had dreams of running even more difficult rivers—the Brahmaputra, the Indus, and other Himalayan rivers—but those too would have to be postponed.

We talked about my Middle Fork trip. Zee recommended July, when the water would be high enough to cover the rocks that had so punished the hulls of his boats in August. June would be too early; the river would be dangerously swollen with water from snow melting in the mountains. He also recommended a party of at least three. He felt certain that Stu Gardiner of Salt Lake City would be interested. That left the necessity of recruiting at least one more person. I tried to find someone at the meeting who would be interested, but virtually everyone had made a commitment to join one or another of the armed forces. A few were already in uniform.

A week later we were at war, and in February I signed up with the Marine Corps. Yale, as well as other universities, had concluded an agreement with the federal government. Students who signed up could finish college, exempt from the draft, and then go directly into officers' training. This made sense. I expected the war to last for a very long time; I thought I might as well complete my education. The plan would even allow me to go forward with my Middle Fork trip, to have one last civilian adventure.

There were many practical problems to solve. What boat should I use? My canoe would swamp in large waves. The homemade boat I had used on the Rapid River was too fragile. Zee recommended a double foldboat, run single. It would be large enough to carry camping gear and food, and if one member of a party of three should lose his boat, there would be an extra seat in either of the other two boats. That was an important consideration when running remote rivers.

I went down to New York to visit Jack Kissner at his small store and workship. Jack sold me one of his standard doubles at a generous discount. The price was about sixty dollars. The boat was seventeen and a half feet long by three feet wide. Skin and frame fitted perfectly. I took out the forward backrest and moved the rear backrest forward to a more central position, which I felt would be better for controlling the boat. This meant that the standard spray cover would no longer fit, but the standard cover was inadequate anyway. Some better method had to be found to close off the nearly seven-foot-long open cockpit. Aside from that remaining problem, I was delighted with the boat.

Early in 1942, one of my college friends volunteered to be the third member of the trip. He was Ed Friedman, a premed student and coxswain of one of the varsity rowing shells. Ed had been canoeing once with me. That was rather slim whitewater experience, but I reasoned that with intensive practice we could sharpen our skills. I too was in need of training. Almost all of my river running had been by canoe, not kayak.

Ed was able to find a good second-hand boat, identical to mine. As was customary among whitewater boaters of the period, we gave our boats names. Mine was the Boriah Eldred, after a sea captain ancestor. Ed's was the Mirkine, after a long-forgotten mathematician. In the same light-hearted spirit, we began calling our venture the DuBois-Friedman Expedition.

On weekends during the spring, we sought out every bit of whitewater that we could find within reach of New Haven. Unfortunately, the winter snowfall had been light, and water levels were low. We got plenty of practice at finding narrow passages between rocks but none at negotiating large waves and powerful currents, conditions we were likely to find on the Middle Fork. Hopefully the West as well as the East had experienced the same lack of snow and rain, and we would find the Middle Fork on the low side. Also, for a June warm-up trip, we planned to run a portion of the Delaware, where we would find more water, even in a dry year.

Late in the spring, there was a development that forced a change of plans. The university and the government worked out an accelerated schedule so that students could graduate early and make a correspondingly early entry into the armed forces. My class was to have graduated in June of 1943, but now we would graduate in December of 1942. Our summer vacation was to be compressed into the month of June, and our senior year was to run from July through December. The Middle Fork trip, if it were to happen at all, would have to be in June, in high water. Ed and I discussed the added risks imposed by this timetable. Our enthusiasm for the adventure and the momentum of our planning made it hard for us to abandon the trip. We decided to go ahead.

We had a great deal to do in a short time. Ed and I started making lists. This was before the days of sporting-goods stores stocked with well-designed lightweight equipment and neatly packaged foods. We took advice where we could get it. At that time I was dating a girl named Lenore. Lenore's mother had definite ideas about what to take on the trip. "What you need as the basis of your diet is something to stick to your ribs—pancakes. Take plenty of pancake flour. Also take a ham; it will keep better than most foods."

Two weeks before leaving for Idaho I solved the problem of the large open cockpits of our foldboats. I devised decks made of very thin plywood, arched to shed water and rimmed by a light frame that fitted snugly over the cockpit coaming. Within this deck there was a small opening for the paddler. Some water could still come through this opening, but I hoped that I had arrived at the right compromise between keeping water out and allowing a quick exit in an emergency.

The last stage of preparation was to consult once more with Zee, now a lieutenant junior grade in the navy and stationed in Washington, D. C. I took the train to Washington. First I went to the Department of the Interior, where I bought a set of maps and profile sheets based on a 1930 survey of the Middle Fork. With my maps in hand, I found my way to Zee's address, which was a yacht basin. Zee and several other young officers were living aboard an ancient motor yacht, the Amorita. Zee and I went to a restaurant for dinner, then returned to the boat, where Zee produced a bottle of Scotch and two glasses. We sat in the lounge of the Amorita and studied maps late into the evening.

Zee identified some of the worst rapids, and I made notations, such as, "bad," "land here," "watch out for log jam," "avoid hermit, right bank." There were suggestions concerning transportation to and from the river, names of people who could be of help, such as Taylor Williams, chief guide at Sun Valley. By midnight I had absorbed all the information I could hold. Zee poured a nightcap, and we toasted the success of my trip. Then I crawled into a bunk. The gentle Potomac lapped at the sides of the Amorita, but I was listening to the roar of the Middle Fork two thousand miles away.

A few days later, I took leave of my family. Worried though they may have been, my parents were supportive of the venture. I had turned twenty in January, and they allowed me to make my own mistakes.

I took the train to New York, spent the night at the Friedmans' house, and the next day went with Ed and his father to Grand Central Station. Ed's father was a delightful person, a successful lawyer, a patron of the arts, but he was definitely a city dweller. It was impossible for him to understand just why his son was running off to Idaho to shoot the rapids of a wilderness river. Over a cup of coffee, I tried to reassure him about the trip. I explained that Zee had gone over the maps with me and had pointed out those places where we should be careful. I felt that I had somewhat reduced Mr. Friedman's fears, when a tall man, dressed in a business suit but wearing cowboy boots and hat, came over to our table and drawled, "I couldn't help but hear what you boys were talking about. You see, I know that section of Idaho very well. It's beautiful country, one of the most rugged parts of the West. As for the Middle Fork of the Salmon, yes sir, it was the strength of my own right arm that saved me from death in that river. I was carrying a load of mining equipment, trying to ford the river, when that terrible current just swept me off my feet."

Mr. Friedman turned pale. "What about animals?" he asked. "Are there any dangerous wild animals?"

"Well, there's one section down there along the Middle Fork where there's more rattlers than anywhere in the West." Then turning to Ed and me, he added, "Boys, it's a mighty dangerous trip you're undertaking, but if you've had lots of experience, you might make it."

The man left. Ed's father urged us to hire a guide. That was not within our budget, and besides, guides competent to run western rivers were scarce. Ed promised that we would use our heads. We finished our coffee, found our way to the train, said good-by to the obviously worried Mr. Friedman, and climbed aboard.

Three days later we got off the train at Shoshone, Idaho. We were dog-tired from sitting up for three nights. Besides being tired, I felt completely out of place, a tenderfoot on a fool's mission. From his glum expression, I suspected that Ed had much the same feelings. Without sharing our thoughts, we gathered our baggage and climbed onto the bus for Sun Valley.

2

Caution to the Wind

The bus, which could hold perhaps a dozen people, headed north across a vast plain covered by sagebrush and punctuated by outcroppings of lava. I remembered reading that this plain, the result of an ancient outflow of molten rock, covered much of southern Idaho. A cock pheasant flew across the road. In the distance, ahead of us, we could see the white peaks of mountains. We knew that somewhere in those mountains lay the Middle Fork. After a great distance, the road penetrated a valley. We came to the town of Ketchum and then turned off to the right for the short drive to Sun Valley, which at that time was fresh and new, a small cluster of handsome buildings set near a willow-lined creek and among hills that were bare except for sagebrush and bunchgrass, the same hills that today are covered by an infestation of condominiums.

Ed and I checked in at the desk of the Challenger Inn and found that Stu Gardiner was waiting for us. Stu was tall, thin, and rugged. It was reassuring to me that the third member of our group was so obviously capable and had had a background of camping and river running in the West. Stu greeted us warmly but let us know right away that there was a problem. The rivers and creeks around Salt Lake were all in flood, and the same was probably true in central Idaho. We sought out Taylor Williams, chief guide at Sun Valley and hunting and fishing companion of Ernest Hemingway. Taylor was a short, dark-haired man with a neatly trimmed moustache and a well-pressed lumberjack shirt. He greeted us cordially with his slightly southern accent. Zee had written him about our proposed trip, so Taylor was expecting us. He confirmed Stu's supposition.

"All the rivers in Idaho are at flood stage," he said. "There was a deep snow accumulation in the mountains during the winter, and it started to melt all at once. On top of that, we've had a lot of rain. I've heard of three drownings from the high water already."

"Were those people running the rivers?" I asked.

"No," said Taylor. "In one case it was from trying to cross a river in one of those little hand-pulled cable cars. Those things are usually fifteen or twenty feet above the river, but in this case the water was so high it tipped over the car, and a woman and a child were spilled into the water, and of course they drowned."

"That sounds bad," I said, "but do you have any specific information on the Middle Fork?"

"Bound to be like the rest," said Taylor.

I felt sick. After all our preparations and two thousand miles of travel, we were to be stopped by a chance combination of thaw and rain.

"Look," I said. "It's only June 12. If we wait a week, perhaps the water will go down enough to make the river runnable."

Stu shook his head. "I have a problem there. My bosses at the bank think I'm crazy to be running rivers. They were very reluctant to let me go. I talked them into letting me have two weeks. If we wait a week, then there will be only one week to go down the river and for me to get back to Salt Lake. That's not enough time."

"Why don't you go over and run the Boise?" Taylor suggested. "It isn't as dangerous as the Middle Fork Salmon, but you'd still have a good time."

"Is there any way we could take a look at the Middle Fork and, if it looked too bad, switch over to the Boise?" I asked.

"Sure," said Stu. "We could drive up to Bear Valley, hike down into the canyon, and see what it looks like."

That's what we decided to do. We couldn't leave immediately because the spray decks, which had been shipped express, hadn't yet arrived. We filled the time by working on our equipment. Later, we climbed into Stu's old Chevrolet and drove the one mile to Ketchum.

Ketchum had been a mining center in the 1860s, and in 1942 it still had an authentic western flavor. It was a small settlement with a few stores and more than a few taverns stretched out along the north-south road. We went into one of the stores and bought supplies. Here is the list we used on that day:

Dried Apricots & Dried Prunes
Bisquick 1 package
Corn Meal Pancake Flour   Take different kinds   2 boxes
Can of Maple Syrup
3 lb Coffee (35 cups to the lb) save eggshells
sweet chocolate   24 bars
3½ lb bacon   (save bacon fat)
3 doz eggs   (already have one)
8 or 9 lbs ham
boxes cereal   1 box cream of wheat
~~maybe canned milk~~
3 cans fruit juice
6 cans baked beans

ketchup
4 cans corned beef
salt
matches
10 lbs potatoes   (old for baking)
3 lbs onions
2 lbs butter
(whiskey—quart)
honey—quart
lots of Matches

Stu dissuaded us from buying quite everything on this formidable list, but we ended up with about sixty pounds of food for the twelve days that we estimated it would take to reach and to run the river. We also bought film, trout flies, and salmon eggs—though I protested that I would use them only as a last resort—and we bought fishing licenses.

After we were through with the store, we went into one of the taverns, a substantial log-cabin structure. It was dark and cool inside, with a long, highly polished bar. On the bar was a roulette wheel, and on the wall in back of the bar were the stuffed heads of all the game animals of Idaho: bear, mountain lion, mountain sheep, mountain goat, antelope, elk, and mule deer. One of the mule deer heads supported a set of antlers with so many branchings and points that it looked like a chandelier or a creation of Dr. Seuss. Stu explained that such a rack was a freak, and the next year the animal might have normal antlers.

"Not if he had been previously shot and stuffed," observed Ed.

The next morning the spray decks arrived, so we were free to leave. We checked out of the Challenger Inn and then said good-by to Taylor Williams. He put on a serious face and warned us, "Boys, I don't want to spoil your fun, but I'd like you to realize that the Middle Fork is a dangerous river. Zee ran it late in the summer when the water was down, but this is June, a spring month for us here in central Idaho. This time of year there are places down there on the Middle Fork where the logs just churn around in the current. Nobody cleans out that river, you know."

"I know about logs," said Stu. "I've had two shots at the Middle Fork, and on the second one I smashed my boat on a log."

"Then you know what I'm talking about," said Taylor. "That's good, but I hope you'll be careful."

After that somber message, we squeezed into Stu's car and left Sun Valley. At Ketchum we turned north. The road ran parallel to the Big Wood River, a narrow stream that was raging along, filling its banks. High as it was, the river had been much higher, way over its banks; the water level was dropping. Stu commented on the river. "I don't like running creeks and rivers when they're that high. You move too fast and there are no eddies along the sides, so you can't stop. I've had some bad times running creeks in high water."

The road soon changed from blacktop to gravel. We climbed steadily and after twenty miles wound steeply up to a pass where there was deep snow beside the road. We crossed a narrow ridge and emerged from the forest to face a tremendous view. This was Galena Summit, 8,700 feet above sea level. Spread out below us and away to the north was a broad valley. Its floor was a flat expanse of grassland with a small stream winding through the middle. That stream was the beginning of the Main Salmon River. The right side of the valley was blocked from view, but on the left we saw a panorama of forests, foothills, and then mountains—a long row of sharp peaks, streaked with snow.

"You're looking at Stanley Basin," said Stu, "and the mountains are the Sawtooth Range."

The name was well chosen, for the peaks succeeded one another like the teeth of a saw. Stu talked excitedly about the prospect of climbing there. He had recently taken up rock climbing, though this activity was viewed with just as much suspicion as whitewater boating by the officials of the bank where he worked.

"I don't see that it's any of their business what you do in your spare time," I said.

"You don't know Salt Lake," said Stu gloomily.

We descended through a series of switchbacks and drove thirty miles down the valley to a place where the Salmon, now a respectable river, turned to the east through a narrow opening in the hills. To the west was the town of Stanley, beautifully situated against a backdrop of the Sawtooth Range. Stanley consisted of about a dozen log cabins, most of them taverns. We stopped at a small gas station. Stu asked the owner about the road to Bear Valley.

"Blocked by snow; you'd never be able to get through."

That was discouraging news. "Is there any other way to get in to the Middle Fork?" I asked Stu.

"There's Marsh Creek," he said. "It's small and steep and as far as I know it's never been run, but as long as we're here, we might as well have a look at it."

We drove west on a narrow dirt road, so unused that in places grass grew between the tire tracks. Crossing a marshy meadow, we stuck fast in mud, an experience familiar to me from driving New England roads in the spring. Ed and I pushed while Stu applied that sensitive pressure on the gas pedal that provides traction without spinning the wheels. As we pushed, we were at the mercy of swarms of mosquitoes. We pushed harder, and the car reached the far side of the mudhole.

Twenty miles from Stanley, we reached Marsh Creek, stopped at a bridge, and looked down at the water. It filled the banks and moved along at a good clip. We could tell that the creek had been even higher because grass in the low spots of the meadow beside the creek had been laid flat by the just-passed flood. In spite of the velocity of the water, there was nothing threatening about the creek. It wound through a pleasant valley bottom, open meadow except for clumps of spruce.

The creek headed in the direction of a notch in the hills, but before it reached the notch, it disappeared into the forest.

We left the car to scout downstream on foot. Stu knew that a trail followed the creek, but he couldn't remember on which side. We followed the right bank but soon were blocked by another creek which came in from the right. This was Beaver Creek, and it appeared to be carrying about as much water as Marsh. In my eagerness to see what lay downstream, I waded into Beaver Creek. The footing was bad, and the swift water was up to my thighs, but I got across. I turned to see Stu and Ed standing on the bank, obviously not intending to follow. They shouted that they would go back to the car and set up the boats while I continued scouting. I scrambled down the bank, sometimes following faint game trails. I startled four mule deer. At times I spashed through beaver ponds that dammed up small side creeks. The canyon became increasingly narrow and steep-sided, slide-rock alternating with timber-covered slopes. Higher up, there were rock walls and pinnacles, terrain very different from anything I'd been used to. One outcropping of rock came down into the creek. To get past this obstacle, I eased myself down into the cold water and worked my way around the rock, hanging on with my fingers. Halfway around, I realized I was being very foolish; I might be dragged out into the current. Reversing the process, going upstream, would be almost impossible. Fortunately, that wasn't necessary. A quarter-mile downstream I found a crude log bridge across the creek. To this point, the trail had been on the far side, but now it continued down the right bank.

So far the creek had been swift but, in my view, easily negotiable by foldboat. There were no large waves, no serious problems of rock-dodging. As for the bridge, it was just high enough to slip under.

I continued down the trail for at least two more miles as the creek grew progressively steeper. There was an island, around the left side of which a channel carried most of the water through a tangle of downed trees. These were not logs left over from some lumbering operation, but trees undercut from the bank or swept into the creek by landslide or avalanche. The channel to the right of the island was clear, though it carried less water and some rocks broke the surface.

Below the island, the trail passed through a stand of tall spruce while the creek swung away to the left, to the far side of an alder thicket and up against the slide-rock of the canyon wall. Then creek and trail came together, the creek cutting sharply to right and left, dropping steeply. Finally, I came to a place where a landslide, many years past, had filled the canyon with broken rock. The remains of this old slide formed a hill in the center of the canyon and blocked my view downstream. The creek had forced a passage close to the right canyon wall. Here the water swirled in a big eddy by the right bank, then plunged over a sharp drop and went out of sight around a corner to the left. At the same place, the trail disappeared under water, and I could see no way of going farther on foot.

It was late afternoon, and with nothing to eat since breakfast in Sun Valley, I decided to turn back. The big eddy would be a good place to stop if we decided to run the creek. I tied my handkerchief to an alder bush so that I could easily identify the eddy as I came around the corner upstream. On the way back to the car, a distance of about four miles, I avoided most of the hazards I'd encountered on the way down by crossing on the footbridge and following the trail up the other bank.

It was dark by the time I reached the car. Ed and Stu were inside, driven there by mosquitoes. I climbed in, and we had a conference, sharing our experiences of the afternoon. After leaving me at Beaver Creek, Stu and Ed had gone back upstream to the road bridge, crossed over, found the trail, and scouted downstream for only a mile. They had seen one beaver and plenty of fast water.

"It is fast," I admitted, "and the water level is certainly high, but I haven't seen anything more difficult than a lot of stuff I've run. About four miles downstream there's a big eddy on the right, a good stopping place. Perhaps we can run that far. If we find the water is too tough for us, we can carry out. If we can handle it okay, we can keep on going."

Stu's better judgment was in favor of leaving immediately for the Boise, but he had made two unsuccessful attempts to run the Middle Fork, and he dearly wanted a third chance. He agreed to my plan.

We asked Ed how he felt about it.

"It looks awfully wild to me," he said, "but you fellows know much more about it than I do, so you decide."

We found a good camping spot, built a fire, cooked and ate supper. We spread out our sleeping bags and turned in. I was comfortable at first but soon realized that my sleeping bag, adequate enough for northern Maine in August, was not up to this nearly 7,000-foot altitude in central Idaho in June. I slept very little. Ed, who had picked up a slight cold on the train, was even more uncomfortable.

In the morning, we cooked breakfast and then began to assemble our boats. Foldboat manufacturers claimed that their products could be assembled in ten minutes, but I found thirty minutes a minimum. A few problems with the frame or the fit of the skin could drag this out to an hour. Boats assembled, we stowed our duffle bags and other gear, tying every item in, to minimize loss in case of an upset. When the boats were loaded, it was obvious that Ed and I were carrying too much, so we sacrificed some items and left them in Stu's car. We put on life jackets. We wore no helmets or wet-suits, it being long before they were available or in common use. By the time we were ready to go, it was noon.

3

And Then There Was One

Looking back at that scene, it's easy to see that everything that had happened up to that point was contributing to a potential disaster. Everything had gone wrong: the accelerated school year, forcing the trip into June; the low water in the East, limiting Ed's and my practice sessions; the unusually high water in Idaho; Stu's limited vacation; the snow blocking the road to Bear Valley; our separation while scouting the creek, so that Ed and Stu relied on my over-optimistic judgment. The rational thing to have done would have been to admit that circumstances were too much for us and to have packed up and left. Our mistake, or rather mine because I was the chief instigator, was of a type made over and over again, not only by whitewater boaters, but by mountain climbers, sailors, participants in all sorts of potentially hazardous sports and ventures. The investment of time, money, and enthusiasm in a particular project is so strong that it's hard to turn back, even when all common sense shouts out that to go on could easily bring tragic results.

Perhaps some small part of me was listening to those inner warnings because I still recall the tight feeling in the pit of my stomach as I eased into the cockpit of my boat. Still, it was difficult to picture anything bad happening on such a beautiful day. The sun was shining. The grass beside the creek was fresh and green. Beyond the meadows were dark forests and

the foothills of mountains. Altogether, it was a picture-postcard scene, "Beautiful Idaho; wish you were here."

As we pushed off from the bank, I took the lead because I had scouted as far as the big eddy. Ed came second, the appropriate place for the least experienced in a three-boat party. Stu brought up the rear. We had agreed that when we reached the Middle Fork, he would take over the lead, and thereafter he and I would alternate. We drifted with the current, first through the meadow past occasional clumps of spruce. The clumps grew more frequent, and soon both banks were forested. Beaver Creek came in on the right, and at the same time, the valley narrowed.

The river, for as an easterner I would classify it as a river, reminded me of the upper Shepaug or the Bantam, neither overly challenging, but I had to admit that we were moving quite fast and there were few eddies in which to stop. I glanced back. Ed and Stu were following and having no problems. Rounding a bend, I passed within a boat-length of three deer. We slid down straight stretches, negotiated bends on the inside, often backpaddling to give time to maneuver. Much sooner than I expected, we came to the bridge. I passed between two rocks and slid under the logs that formed the bridge just at the spot I had picked out the evening before. Ed and Stu followed my path exactly. We continued for several miles down a stream that progressively picked up speed and more and more came to resemble a sluiceway, having no eddies along the banks.

We came to the island. I headed for the right channel, but before I could enter it, I caught the bow of my boat and spun around. This caused a near pileup of the three boats because Ed and Stu had been running too close behind me. I broke free of the rock and went through the chute backward. At the bottom of the chute, I jammed the stern against the right bank and let the current swing the boat around so that I was again headed downstream. Before rounding the next bend, I glanced upstream and saw Stu walking down the bank and Ed, in his boat, coming down the chute. A quarter-mile farther on, I found a long eddy on the left side of the creek. I swung into the eddy, and shortly Ed pulled in beside me. Ed was excited.

"This is terrific, isn't it!" he said.

"Yeah."

"I've got some water in my boat," Ed said.

"So have I," I answered, "but this isn't a good place to land."

We were at the bottom of a talus slope, the water lapping at the sides of great boulders. Although it wouldn't have been easy, we could have found a place to land and bail out the boats. That would have been the wise thing to do because a load of water shifting back and forth inside a boat makes it unstable, but I was thinking of the convenience of pulling ashore at the big eddy downstream.

"Look," I said, "there's a big eddy against the right bank about a half-mile below here. It's a good place to land. How about it?"

"Lead and I follow."

I pushed my bow into the current and was off like a shot. I was soon in so much trouble that there was no time to look back to check on Ed. The water was overflowing the banks of the creek, the grade was steep, and there were many sharp bends. The boat had to be turned in anticipation of each corner. This meant riding through waves sideways, a tricky balancing job. Finally, I turned a sharp corner to the right, looked down a short pitch where boulders just broke the surface of the water, and below that saw my handkerchief tied to an alder bush. I picked a route between the rocks and drove as hard as I could, diagonally across the creek. I had to get across before being swept over the drop that lay just beyond. The bow caught in the eddy and the boat skidded around to a stop against the bank, heading upstream.

I hopped out of my boat, pulled it partway up on the bank, then stationed myself at the tail of the eddy, near the drop. I was afraid that Ed might not handle his boat aggressively enough to get into the head of the eddy. If he should hit it too far downstream, I might be able to catch his boat and prevent him from going over the drop.

Ed should have been right behind me, but minutes passed without any sign of him. Perhaps he had stopped upstream, but that seemed unlikely as the creek was over its banks and moving very fast. Stopping at any place between the talus slope and this eddy would be very difficult. My anxiety mounted. Then, Ed's boat appeared at the bend upstream. It was bottom-side up. At the head of the pitch, one end caught on a rock. The boat pivoted, freed itself, caught on another rock, pivoted again, and slid in front of me, in midcurrent. Horrified, I wondered if Ed were trapped under his boat, in which case I should hop into mine, get out in midcurrent, and try to rescue him. I'd have to do that while being swept over the drop and into the unknown canyon below. On the other hand, if Ed had gotten free of the cockpit and was upstream, but floating toward me, then it would be better to let his boat go. What to do? I was beginning my move toward my boat when, almost in answer to my question, his boat rolled rightside up, revealing an empty cockpit. The boat went over the drop and disappeared around the bend to the left.

It was some relief to know that Ed hadn't been trapped and was probably upstream, but just then I saw his waterproof matchbox floating in the eddy. I knew that it had been in his pocket because I had advised him to put it there. If the turbulence of the water had turned his pocket inside out, perhaps it had ripped the life jacket off his back. That had happened to Zee Grant in an upset on the Colorado. Perhaps Ed had drowned and his body had already slipped by me underwater. Gripped by these imaginings, and full of guilt at having led my friend into danger, I shouted.

"Ed, Ed!"

There was a faint answer from upstream. I ran up the trail,

and there was Ed, walking toward me. He was the wettest and most bedraggled creature I'd ever seen.

"God, but I'm glad to see you!" I blurted out.

"I'm glad to see you, too."

"I was awfully worried about you," I continued.

"I was a bit worried about myself."

"What happened?"

"Oh, I rolled in a wave on one of those corners. I had a little trouble getting out, but when I did, I struck out for shore. What about the Mirkine?"

I explained that his boat had gone down into the canyon and that it would probably be broken up pretty badly in the rapids. I'd seen it happen before.

"Gee, that's too bad," said Ed. "Is there any chance of finding it?"

"We can look for it later, but I doubt if we will find more than pieces. Right now we've got to locate Stu. He should be here by now."

Leaving Ed to get food and dry clothing out of my duffle bag, I ran up the trail. I scanned the banks of the creek and shouted for Stu. The only answer to my call was the chattering of a squirrel. I reached the island where I had last seen Stu without finding any trace of him. All the anxiety I had felt about Ed was now repeated.

I started back downstream, moving more slowly, searching the banks of the creek with more care, and shouting, "Stu, Stu!"

I thought I heard an echo but then realized that the echo wasn't the same as my call. Stu was answering. I located him sitting on the opposite side of the creek, high on the talus slope above the long eddy where Ed and I had stopped. He had apparently climbed there to find a sun-warmed spot, for he was soaked. Below him was his boat, partially pulled up on a rock, but full of water and somewhat smashed in the middle.

Stu climbed down to the water's edge. We were less than

forty feet apart but had to shout to be heard over the noise of the rapids. I told Stu that Ed had upset but was all right. Then I shouted, "This is no good. We'll have to get out of here."

"Yes!" Stu shouted back with emphasis that carried over the roar of the water.

I judged that Stu might have trouble paddling his broken boat across the river, so I went downstream to get the rope that was stored in my boat. I found that Ed, wet and shivering, had been unable to get a fire started. I had never heard of hypothermia, but I knew that shivering was a bad sign. Getting Ed warm had to take top priority, so I built a fire and made a pot of strong coffee. This seemed to be what Ed needed. Fortified by the coffee, we took the rope and went back upstream. Stu, meanwhile, had bailed out his boat. Even though all the middle framework was broken, he climbed in and very cautiously ferried across the river.

We were at last all on the same piece of ground, and each could tell his story. Stu, after scouting the chute by the island, had climbed back in his boat but had almost immediately run afoul of the same rock that had spun me around, only Stu caught the rock amidships. In whitewater that is the beginning of disaster. His boat turned broadside to the current and tipped upstream. The cockpit dipped under the surface, water poured in, and the whole boat was wrapped around the rock by the pressure of the current. Early in this process, Stu freed himself from the cockpit. He succeeded in getting the boat off the rock, but the current took it down the chute, Stu clinging to the boat with one hand and to his paddle with the other. He slid up on the overturned boat and tried to paddle for shore, but his boat kept rolling underneath him. He was swept downstream for at least a quarter-mile before he could coax the boat into the eddy below the talus slope.

Two out of three boats lost or smashed in less than four miles. My overly optimistic appraisal of the rapids had given our Middle Fork expedition a dismal end. Now we were faced with the task of carrying our boats and gear out of the canyon. We decided that that effort would have to wait for the next day. We found a campsite in a stand of lodgepole pines, the only flat piece of ground in this section of the canyon. A fire circle and some wood that had been cut with an ax indicated that fishermen or hunters had camped there before. We brought all our gear to this spot. Then, leaving Ed to get some much-needed rest, Stu and I hiked downstream.

At the big eddy, Stu solved the problem of the disappearing trail by wading into the water. The trail was still there, three feet under water and at the base of a cliff. After about thirty yards, the trail started to lead out of the water but was blocked by a steep slope of loose gravel, the product of a landslide. We climbed this precarious incline and again found the trail, which now angled up the canyon wall to a height of about two hundred feet above the creek.

This was a wild spot. Across the creek to the south were the rocky buttresses of Cape Horn Mountain. To our right, the north, the canyon wall sloped up, timber covered but very steep. The creek, directly below us, frothed white over many rocks. We spotted a few pieces of Ed's boat: broken bits of plywood floating in eddies, a part of the spray deck against the far bank. Farther downstream, we found a place where a massive landslide had once dammed up the creek. The upstream side of the dam had been silted in, so that there was a less-than-average drop to the streambed. On the downstream side of the slide, the drop was made up in a short distance. The water boiled down over a mass of boulders. Stu and I agreed that the place was unrunnable.

We followed the trail down to the junction with Bear Valley Creek. It was a forbidding place, quite dark in the thick forest and under the shadow of Cape Horn Mountain. Here the two creeks came together to form the Middle Fork. The river was within a small, straight-sided canyon within the larger canyon. I remembered from geology class that this was called "rejuvenation" and was the result of a recent upthrust of this mountainous area.

Bear Valley Creek brought in even more water than Marsh Creek; the combined volume was impressive. Several years before, Stu had kayaked the Main Salmon from North River to the mouth of the Middle Fork, the first person to kayak that stretch of river. He had looked up into the canyon of the Middle Fork and had a general idea of the flow of water at the mouth of the river at that time. Now, 106 miles upstream, Stu said we were looking at a much greater volume of water. What would the rapids of the Impassable Canyon be like under these conditions? We decided that we were fortunate to have cracked up when we did.

On the way back we found a large pile of wooden boxes marked "dynamite." Stu said that the cache must have been left over from the trail-building activities of the Civilian Conservation Corps in the mid-1930s. The CCC had improved old trails and built new sections of trail all along the Middle Fork—except for the Impassable Canyon, through which no trail could be built. To me it seemed irresponsible to have left such a large store of dynamite just sitting in the woods. I was glad that one foldboating friend of mine wasn't along. He delighted in explosions. I could see him stationing himself behind a rock and taking pot shots at this pile of explosives. Fortunately, my friend was already in the army where he could indulge his hobby legitimately.

On the way back upstream, we picked up a few parts of Ed's boat. We retrieved an inner tube that had been stuffed under the deck for flotation. Our most impressive find was the complete skin of the boat, only slightly torn, with a few pieces of frame inside. The water had scooped out everything else.

Back at our campsite, we cooked supper and turned in. We had a cold and wet night, and then a difficult day carrying our gear out of the canyon. The distance was four miles, but we had over three hundred pounds to carry. At places the trail was underwater because of the height of the creek, and at other places the trail was blocked by jumbles of downed logs. At still other places, the pack trail was hard to find, and we had to follow game trails. The weather was another hazard. One minute the sun was shining brightly, but the next minute we were pelted by rain or hail or we were chilled by cold winds. Once, when Ed was walking along the trail where it passed through a stand of lodgepole pine, there was a sudden windstorm, and trees all around him were blown down.

Frequently we saw deer. At one time Stu was resting on a stump when an elk came down the trail. The animal came within fifteen feet and might have come closer, except that Stu whistled. The elk looked up, turned, and bolted at top speed, leaving a splayed-out hoof print where it turned a corner of the trail.

All day we hiked up and down the creek, each at his own pace and each immersed in his own disappointment. Once when I met Ed, he going upstream and I going down for another load, he said, "We'll have to call it the ill-fated DuBois-Friedman Expedition."

In the afternoon, Stu hiked on to Cape Horn Ranch and tried to arrange with the rancher, Slim Hendrick, for a pack animal to help us haul our gear. Unfortunately, all of Slim's pack horses were at Stanley, but Stu did arrange for us to spend the night at Cape Horn, and that was a godsend. Slim's wife Mildred cooked us a wonderful dinner, and we had the luxury of sitting in front of a good fire in the ranch house living room.

After the Hendrick children, two small boys named Mike and Dale, had been put to bed, Slim told us his own Middle Fork horror story. He had been taking a packtrain down the trail that runs along the river. While crossing at one of the fords, he was swept off his horse. The animal scrambled into shallow water and then up the bank, but Slim was carried downstream by the swift current, finally stopping himself by clinging to the face of a cliff that dropped straight into the water. He had only a meager fingerhold on the rock and couldn't pull himself out of the water. All he could do was hang on. After a half-hour, one of the men who was handling the pack animals was able to work his way out on to the cliff, fifty feet up and directly above Slim. The man then lowered a rope, but since Slim couldn't let go of the rock, he first took the rope in his teeth and then in his hands. With the aid of the rope, he reached safety. This experience gave Slim a lasting respect for the Middle Fork.

That night we slept in warm beds, and in the morning we had a filling breakfast. We went back to Marsh Creek with more energy than we'd had the day before. However, it was late afternoon before we had everything out of the canyon and stowed in Stu's car, so we spent one more night at Cape Horn Ranch. In the morning, we said good-by to the hospitable Hendrick family and drove back the way we had come.

We stopped in Stanley for an early lunch. I noticed that the place was empty and asked Stu how the taverns could survive with so few customers.

"On Saturday night, the miners come out of the hills. Places like this get pretty lively," Stu explained.

I walked over to the jukebox to see what it offered. Instead of Glenn Miller and Tommy Dorsey, here was a collection of cowboy songs, performers and titles I'd never heard of, a different world. One big-band tune had bridged the gap. I punched in a nickel, and the machine belted out, "Beyond the hills of Idaho, where yawning canyons greet the sun." It was not one of the biggest hits of the day, but it had an agreeable bounce and was full of open-air nostalgia. Well, we'd seen one of Idaho's yawning canyons, and after yawning it had come close to swallowing us up.

Back in Sun Valley, Ed and I regretfully said good-by to Stu, who headed back to Salt Lake City and his job at the bank. Before he could run any more rivers, he would have to repair his foldboat. Of necessity, whitewater boaters were skilled carpenters.

Ed and I tried to slink into Sun Valley unnoticed, but our attempt on the Middle Fork with its disastrous end was known to everyone in the place even before we arrived. We gave Taylor Williams the details of our story.

He said, "We thought all along you'd run into trouble, but you boys were so eager to run that river, we didn't want to discourage you."

Later, one of the ski instructors came up to me and said, "So, it turned out to be a little too much for you." I don't know what his nationality was, but he had a heavy German accent. The man was wearing his ski boots, wore a silk scarf at his throat, and as far as I could tell, had penciled his eyebrows. He went on. "Too bad. Perhaps next time you'll try something a little less difficult, yes? How would you like to stay in one of our pioneer cabins? They're up in the mountains, very nice, just like being a pioneer, but with all the conveniences."

"Thank you for your suggestion," I said as politely as I could, but I was boiling inside. Besides not liking to be reminded of failure, I was reacting to his accent and his condescending manner.

Ed and I sent telegrams and letters to our families. Then, so as to blend in with the rest of the guests, we put on our good clothes and wandered around to see what there was to do. There was plenty to do, all very nice, very relaxing, very civilized, but not what we'd come to Idaho to experience. If we couldn't run the Middle Fork, at least we'd enjoy a more authentic portion of the West. In the morning, we put in a call to Slim Hendrick and asked if he could drive down to Sun Valley and take us back to his ranch for the rest of our stay in Idaho. He said he could. Then Ed and I made our return train reservations, his for June 26, to be in time for his first term at Harvard Medical School, mine for July 2, to start my senior year at Yale.

When Slim drove up to the Challenger Inn, we were waiting for him. We left some of our belongings at Sun Valley but brought along my boat, folded in its two bags. I reasoned that we might find a lake to fish or an easy river to run. As an after-thought, I strapped the spray deck to the outside of the car. Once again, we drove over Galena Summit and enjoyed the tremendous view into Stanley Basin. When we reached Cape Horn Ranch, it was after dark. Mildred Hendrick had supper ready. We ate at the kitchen table and found that much more agreeable than sitting in the dining room at the Challenger Inn.

Ed and I had a great time at Cape Horn Ranch. About a mile from the ranch house, there was a small lake where I caught a fourteen-inch Dolly Varden trout. One day Slim saddled up three horses. He, Ed, and I rode up Lola Creek, a small tributary of Marsh Creek that flows down the flank of Cape Horn Mountain. We caught no fish that day, but the country was beautiful. Most of the time, we relaxed around the ranch house. We ate very well. I remember an excellent peach pie, baked by Mildred. Ed and I praised the pie lavishly. Slim seemed embarrassed. He said, "Oh, she does pretty well," which must have been high praise from the way Mildred looked down and smiled. Evenings, we sat in front of the fire listening to Slim tell of one experience or another. He fretted about the fireplace, said it was too deep to give much heat for the wood burned, but Ed and I enjoyed it. Time passed so pleasantly that the Middle Fork and our misadventure on Marsh Creek were almost forgotten.

One day while Ed and I were off fishing, the Oregon river guide Woodie Hindman stopped at the ranch on his way to the Middle Fork. Having run the river several times since 1939, he was now back again with another guide and a few paying pas-sengers. This was the earliest in the season that he had at-tempted the river, but he wanted to try it under conditions of high water. The road to Bear Valley was by now free of snow, so Hindman would be able to launch his McKenzie boats at the usual place and run down Bear Valley Creek.

Hindman and his group were gone by the time Ed and I got back to the ranch. Slim told us about Hindman's plans. Instantly my interest in the Middle Fork was rekindled. I saw a means of salvaging my wrecked ambition to run the river. I would assemble my boat, start down Marsh Creek, join Hindman, and continue with his party on down the Middle Fork. I knew that running any whitewater alone was very hazardous but reasoned that I'd only be running Marsh Creek alone. If Hindman started down Bear Valley Creek the next morning, and if I started down Marsh Creek at the same time, we would arrive simultaneously at the junction of the two creeks. This scheme appealed to me so much that I gave no thought at all as to whether Hindman would agree to let me go along with him down the river.

When I unfolded this plan to Ed and Slim, they both told me I was crazy. We got into a long debate. I pointed out that the water level would surely be lower and therefore safer than when Ed, Stu, and I made our first attempt. I also said that if I failed to make contact with Hindman or had any other problems, I could always abandon my boat and hike back along the trail. When I was through with those arguments, Ed had one comment:

"I think you're nuts, just plain nuts."

"Granted," I said, "but this is what I want to do."

Slim, seeing that I had absolutely made up my mind, helped me plan what I should take with me. He was used to travel in wilderness areas, by horse rather than by boat, and he had a good feel for what was essential and what wasn't. A lot of equipment had been lost in Ed's boat, but there was an advantage in this loss, because it helped me to conserve weight. For this second attempt on the river, my mess kit consisted of one small frying pan and one large tin can that could be used both for cooking and for bailing out the boat. For food, I took: four-and-a-half pounds of ham; one-fourth pound of bacon; one-eighth pound of butter; one-half pound of cheese; six eggs; eight beef soup cubes; one pound of honey; five pounds of pancake flour; three-fourths pound of coffee. I had two sets of clothes: one set to wear on the river with the expectation that it would be wet most of the time; another dry set for staying warm after I made camp. I had my life jacket, my sleeping bag, an air mattress, and a poncho. I carried maps, matches, and toilet paper. Slim claimed that this last item was unnecessary, but I took it anyway. I carried three other items of debatable value and all rather heavy: a .22-caliber pistol, my trail ax, and a 16-mm movie camera. All this was fitted into my waterproof duffle bag, which was tied to the bottom frame of the boat, between my legs. Inside the boat I also carried my fishing rod, a spare paddle, an 80-foot length of rope, plus inflated inner tubes to give buoyancy in case of an upset. The inner tubes were lent to me by Slim. In my pockets, I carried bars of tropical chocolate, plus matches in a waterproof box. On my belt I wore a sheath knife, my only utensil. The total weight of all these supplies and items of equipment came to about seventy-five pounds. The boat weighed another seventy-five. Spray deck and paddle added about fifteen pounds. The total: one hundred and sixty-five pounds, just equal to my own weight at the time.

With all preparations made and supper over, I went to bed. I was in a peculiar mood, elated because of my chance to run the Middle Fork, but depressed because I knew Ed was right when he said I was nuts. It took a long time for me to fall asleep. In the morning, Mildred prepared the biggest breakfast I've ever eaten. There were steaks, ham, bacon, lots of eggs, home-fried potatoes, and mounds of pancakes.

I said good-by to Mildred and thanked her for her hospitality. I also took leave of the two small boys. Ed, Slim, and I got into Slim's car for the short drive to Marsh Creek. Ed was very glum as I set up my boat, stowed the duffle bag and other equipment, and slid the boat into the water. I attempted to reassure him.

"Look, the water's down quite a bit, perhaps a foot."

"Doesn't look much different to me," he grumbled.

We said good-by. Ed's last comments to me were, "I still

think you're nuts, but I sure hope you make it. Have a good time."

I thanked Slim for all his help. He had some last-minute advice.

"Along the middle part of the river there are cabins about every fifteen miles; miners, small ranchers, or people just living off the land. Any one of them would be glad to help you if you need it. There's a friend of mine a few miles beyond Mar-

ble Creek, on the left; name is Milt Hood. Stop off and see him; tell him I sent you. Of course, there's no one in the Impassable Canyon except that hermit, if he's still there, and I think you want to stay away from him. Remember, if you spill in the Impassable Canyon, hang onto your boat. That's the only way you can get out of there."

"I'll remember that," I promised.

I pushed off from shore. Slim walked downstream a few paces to get a picture of me with his camera. As I drifted by with the current he said, "God dammit, supper's at 7:30. Don't be late."

4

The Middle Fork

Feeling more alone than I had ever felt in my life, I slipped along with the current as it wound through the meadow toward the edge of the forest and toward the entry to the canyon. The date was June 22, eight days since our first attempt on Marsh Creek. In the interval, the water had dropped one foot, with the result that more rocks were showing at the surface. The rocks had to be avoided, but they slowed down the water, making the run easier, or at least safer. One rock did cause me a problem; I broke one of my paddle blades on it. I got into an eddy and exchanged the broken paddle for the spare, which was inside the boat.

The spare was the paddle I had used on the Rapid River. I had considered it too short for a foldboat, but I soon found I was better off using it because it brought my paddle strokes closer to the boat. Modern kayakers have taken a lesson from the Eskimos, who use a short paddle, but most early fold-boaters used a paddle that was too long. I used paddle blades that were spooned. The blades were long, narrow, and easily broken. I fitted the two halves of the paddle together so that the blades were parallel rather than feathered, which is the current practice.

After changing paddles, I pushed off into the current and in succession slid past the bridge, the island, the long eddy under the talus slope, and then the sharp corners where Ed had spilled. With the water level down, the velocity was less and the waves were smaller. Negotiating the corners was less precarious than on the first run. Of course, I had the advantage that comes from making a second run, like the second run in whitewater slalom. Those corners would be easier still with a modern slalom kayak, designed to make abrupt turns. My heavily laden, seventeen-and-a-half-foot-long, straight-keeled boat was much more difficult to turn, though at the time I thought my craft the last word in maneuverability.

I landed in the big eddy, the end point of my first run. I pulled the boat on shore, untied my duffle bag, and heaved it onto my shoulder. I had decided to carry it down the trail to the junction of the two creeks. This would lighten the load of the boat and at the same time give me the opportunity to look over that portion of the creek I hadn't yet run. As I hiked downstream, the trail climbed high up the side of the canyon, giving me a good view of the water. The creek was wider and therefore shallower than it was upstream. Many rocks churned the surface with white plumes, too many rocks to make picking a path easy. This was the section that had chewed up Ed's boat; I knew it would be tough.

When I reached the junction, I dropped my duffle bag at a spot where I could easily find it. Then I looked out over the beginning of the Middle Fork and up Bear Valley Creek. There was no sign of Hindman and his party. Back I went upstream, looking over the water a second time, memorizing as much as I could.

Feeling a bit uneasy, I settled myself into the cockpit, pushed the bow out of the eddy, let the current swing the boat around, and went over the drop. I almost flipped over, which was disturbing because the drop hadn't looked that tricky. Then I rounded a corner to the left, went over another drop and into a mass of whitewater thrown up by rocks all across the creek and as far downstream as I could see. Dodging these rocks required instant decision making and quick paddle work because the current was so swift. I made one miscalculation; the bow caught on a rock and I was spun around and went downstream backward. No matter, I looked over my shoulder and continued to maneuver until I could put my stern in an eddy behind a rock. The current straightened me out again, and I continued through the rock garden.

The current slackened; I had reached the upstream side of the landslide. I landed and carried around the unrunnable chute. The boat was an awkward load, and I was glad to get it back in the water to complete the run down to the junction, where I landed, pulled the boat up on shore, and inspected the bottom. There was a small scrape where I'd caught the bow on the rock, but aside from that there was no damage.

I realized that I was probably the first person to run Marsh Creek, but the thought didn't particularly cheer me because I was lonely and a bit scared. Hindman's party was nowhere in sight. I had thought they might camp here at the junction. Perhaps they had come by this point earlier in the day and were on their way to the falls, ten miles downriver. Perhaps they were still coming down Bear Valley Creek. Whatever the case, making contact with Hindman was not as easy as I had imagined. I thought of Marsh Creek, the six tough miles I had come down. I thought of the Middle Fork, stretching one hundred and six miles from this point and much tougher than Marsh Creek or anything else I'd ever been on. I thought of all the warnings and horror stories I'd heard about the river. I was the greatest fool alive to be in this dark and forbidding spot, at the beginning of an undertaking I was ill prepared to complete. It was afternoon. Mildred Hendrick would soon be cooking on the big wood stove in the neat kitchen at Cape Horn Ranch. If I hurried, I could get back just in time for supper at 7:30.

Enough of that, I thought. I'd spend the night here and decide what to do in the morning. I climbed the bank, located my duffle bag, and found a place to camp in the shelter of some large rocks. I built a good fire and cooked my supper: beef bouillon; a slice of ham fried in the pan; an egg, also fried; a couple of pancakes, which I succeeded in tossing when they needed to be turned. I ate the pancakes with a little butter and honey. Finally, I boiled coffee in the boat-bailing can. I settled the grounds with the eggshell and drank the coffee from the same can. Perhaps it wasn't as good a meal as was on the table at Cape Horn, but it was good enough to revive my spirits.

Before turning in, I stripped off all my clothes and checked my entire body for ticks, possible carriers of Rocky Mountain spotted fever. Stu Gardiner had had the disease, and his description of it was unpleasant in the extreme. He advised stripping and looking for ticks at least once a day. Slim Hendrick had a different opinion. He thought that because I was an easterner, I would have such tender skin that I would undoubtedly feel any tick that ventured to crawl on me. A westerner, with tougher and less sensitive skin, would have to check more often. I doubted that nerve endings varied much with longitude, and so I followed Stu's advice. During my stay in Idaho, I found only one tick and he was on his prospecting tour; he hadn't started to dig.

That night started well. I was warm enough in my dry set of clothes and in my sleeping bag. The air mattress kept me off the cold ground, rocks protected me from the wind, and I was as close as was prudent to the embers of the fire. Working against me was the altitude, 6,182 feet, high enough to be very cold at night, even in June. Also working against me was a slow leak in my air mattress, which as the night wore on dropped me onto the ground with only the protection of my kapok sleeping bag. I grew colder and colder, until by morning I was stretched out in my sleeping bag, stiff as a board, not shivering, but close to it. At least I had slept well during the first part of the night, not even bothered by a small animal scurrying across my sleeping bag.

Prompted by the cold, I got up early and built a big fire. Breakfast was a near repeat of supper, except that I skipped the bouillon and ham and had bacon instead. With the new day, I felt much more optimistic. I got out my maps and my river profile charts. Ten miles downstream from this point, the river plunged over a fifteen-foot falls. If Hindman were ahead of me on the river, and that seemed likely, perhaps the process of portaging his boats around the falls would slow him down enough for me to catch up. It seemed worth a try.

I studied the map and the profile of the river. The map showed that between this spot and the falls the river took many sharp bends. From the profile chart, I knew that the average drop was fifty feet per mile, a respectable drop. One mile had a drop of eighty feet, the steepest mile on the Middle Fork, and certain to be a place where rocks and waves would be coming at me very fast.

Studying the map was one thing, but studying the actual water was another. I started down the trail along the right bank, looking down into the water below me. The character of this river was drastically different from Marsh Creek. Boulders were larger; waves were bigger; drops were more abrupt; eddies along the bank were more powerful. Picking a route would be easier in this water, but following the route safely would require a lot of care. As I scouted the river, I kept an eye out for a good eddy in which to land. After two hundred yards, I located one. I memorized the configuration of the banks at this landing spot so that I wouldn't overshoot it and then I hiked back upstream, studying the river once more to be sure I had my route in mind.

Full of anxiety, I tied my duffle bag into the boat, lowered the boat into the water, fitted the spray deck in place, climbed in, and got myself well braced. My feet were against one cross rib. My knees pushed out against another. My buttocks were wedged between two cross members of the boat's keel structure, an uncomfortable but secure seat. My back was against a firm backrest. I was almost a part of the boat. I pushed my paddle against the bank, and drifted into the current of the Middle Fork.

At first cautiously, but then with more confidence, I followed my predetermined course. I edged by a large wave and then dropped past a boulder. Downstream from the boulder there was a large eddy. I anchored my paddle blade in the eddy and drew the boat over into the slower water, giving me time to think about the next drop ahead. At the bottom of the drop I smashed through a standing wave, water sliding across the spray deck, against my life jacket, into my face, pouring down into the cockpit. I was soaked. Ahead of me, a wave angled out from a rock abutment that protruded from the cliff on the right bank. I nearly rolled in that wave. In the next diagonal wave, I did better. I stabilized the boat with a strong paddle stroke on the opposite side. I was learning a rudimentary paddle brace.

When I came to my landing spot, I swung into the eddy and up to the bank. I eased out of the cockpit, transferring my weight onto a rock, then reached back into the boat to bail out the water that had poured in with the big wave. When the boat was reasonably dry, I slid it up on a flat rock and climbed the steep bank to the trail.

As I walked down the trail, looking over the next stretch of water, I carried and referred to Sheet D of the 1930 river survey map. The map didn't tell me anything about the rapids but it did show every twist of the river and every side creek. With it I could keep track of my progress very accurately. This was important because of the falls downstream. I didn't want any nasty surprises.

When I had scouted this next section, I went back to my boat, negotiated the rapids down to the new stopping place, landed, bailed out the boat, climbed the bank, and looked over the next section. Repeating this process, I slowly worked my way downriver, walking nearly twice as far as I traveled by boat. Sometimes I could do my scouting from the trail on the right side of the river, but at other times I could get a better look by scrambling along the opposite bank. In either case the footing was bad, a steep slope on the left bank, an equally steep slope on the right, which had the doubtful advantage of a trail that was often just a furrow blasted out of the broken rock of the talus slope. I realized that the river wasn't my only hazard. I had to guard against a fall while on shore.

At times I could short-cut the scouting process. If there were no obvious hazards ahead, I would climb as high as possible for a good look downstream to pick out my route and to locate an eddy where I could land. Occasionally, I would be swept past my landing point and would have to run a quarter- or half-mile without any previous scouting, looking ahead from river level to find the best path through rocks and waves, and at the same time looking for a good eddy against the bank.

Once, when swept past my landing spot and around a bend to the left, I found myself bearing down on a log that was wedged between rocks. The log blocked the right two-thirds of the river. This was probably the log that had wrecked Stu's boat the previous year. The main current, thrown to the outside of the bend, foamed over the log. I pointed the bow of my boat to the left and paddled with all my strength, just missing the log's end. If I had headed into the corner just two feet more to the right, it would have been a disaster. I landed a short way below, quite shaken by my close call.

This first section of the Middle Fork was teaching me a good deal. Among other things, I was learning how to land in the smallest possible eddy. In continuous rapids, you can't land a boat against the bank except in an eddy, which bears the same relationship to a river as a landing strip to the sky. In both cases, it's vital to know the technique of landing. From my canoeing experience, I knew how to slide close to an eddy and with a sideways push of the paddle, move the stern of my boat into quiet water, letting the bow be pushed in by the current. On the Middle Fork, with its high velocity and small pocket eddies, if there were eddies at all, I found that the bow-first technique was more effective. I didn't go into the eddy with the graceful Duffek turn of modern kayakers, in which the paddle is held nearly vertical and far out to the side of the boat, acting as a pivot about which kayaker and kayak spin gracefully into the eddy. The technique had not yet been developed, and my equipment would not have been suitable for it. Rather, I plunged the bow of my boat into the head of the eddy and stabilized with my paddle as best I could as the boat snapped around.

After my close encounter with the log, I decided it was time for lunch, a piece of cheese that I had put in my shirt pocket. I was so keyed up that I couldn't have eaten anything more.

I went back to working my way downstream. Knowing that the falls were ahead, I paid close attention to the map. It had a good scale but showed only the contours of the first three hundred feet up the canyon sides, whereas the walls themselves were between seven hundred and a thousand feet high. The maps had been made to determine the locations of possible dams; for that purpose the higher contour lines were unimportant, but for me they would have been a great help. I couldn't spot a pinnacle of rock and identify it on that map.

Toward the end of the afternoon, I came to a place where the canyon wall on the left swung briefly away from the river. According to the map, this was where Dagger Creek came in, in which case the falls were just ahead. At that time the falls were called Salmon Falls or sometimes Sulfur Falls. The name

Salmon Falls was perhaps given because of the name of the river or because this was an easy spot to spear salmon as they made their upstream run to spawn in Bear Valley and Marsh creeks. The name Sulfur Falls came from Sulfur Creek, which enters the Middle Fork two miles beyond the falls and which is the largest creek in the immediate area. Later, the name was changed to Dagger Falls, after the creek that comes into the river a short distance above the falls. Dagger Falls it is today.

Falls and rapids in a river are often named for the nearest tributary creek. In the names of creeks is written much of the history of the West. The Middle Fork has a number of side creeks that are suggestive of a lively past. Marsh Creek is named for the meadows at its headwaters, choked with beaver ponds when Hudson's Bay Company trappers first saw it early in the last century. Bear Valley Creek is named for the bears that scooped salmon from its spawning beds. I don't know the origin of the name Dagger Creek, but perhaps it relates to a series of creeks farther downstream that are named for every weapon known in the late nineteenth century, from Cannon Creek to Peashooter Creek. Another series of creeks celebrates the horns and antlers of game animals: Elkhorn Creek, Ramshorn Creek, and Velvet Creek, this last named for the velvet stage of deer antlers. Boundary Creek, just downstream from Dagger Falls, was the boundary between sheep country and cattle country. Sulfur Creek is named for the hot sulfur springs along its banks. Camas Creek is named for the camas root, once a staple of Indian diet. Color Creek reflects the glint of gold at the bottom of a prospector's pan, as does Nugget Creek. Papoose Creek immortalizes a night when a detachment of the U. S. Army was kept awake by the howling of an Indian baby. The past of other creeks may not be so well known, but each has a story reflecting its importance to Indian, trapper, miner, traveler, stockman, or soldier.

After passing Dagger Creek I was particularly cautious and found a safe landing spot well above the falls. I pulled into shore beside a patch of sand in which I saw the fresh imprint of a boot. Hindman was ahead of me, not behind. It was possible that he was just ahead, still making his portage around the falls. I had landed on the right bank. As quickly as possible, I climbed to the trail and ran downstream, crossing the river on a crude suspension bridge just above the falls. A hundred and fifty yards downstream and at the bottom of a steep slope was the obvious launch site. No one was there, nor could I see any boats downstream. I was too late.

I had wanted to spend the night at Sulfur Creek. Zee had advised me that a dip in one of the hot springs would do wonders for sore muscles. Mine ached, and I felt cold as well. I went back to my boat, took out the duffle bag, and then started to carry the boat up the bank and downstream around the falls. It was a heavy load, and I began to question the wisdom of completing the portage and then going the two extra miles to Sulfur Creek that evening. Running ten miles and dropping five hundred feet had been a tough day's work. In two days, I had dropped nearly a thousand feet. More taxing than the physical effort had been the constant need to make no mistakes in water that was clearly above my skill level. I had been alarmed by my close call with the log and by the two or three moments of similar hazard when I was nearly flipped over by the waves. In truth, I had been scared almost continually. The ground at Dagger Falls felt reassuringly solid under my feet.

The falls, with its fifteen-foot drop, was an impressive sight. In two steps the water tumbled into a small box canyon and surged along between perpendicular rock walls. On the east bank, the canyon rose steeply for over a thousand feet. On the west side, and just above the inner canyon, there was a stand of pines on level ground. Then the canyon wall climbed, but it was neither as steep nor as high as on the east bank. A vertical slab of rock separated the gorge from the level ground. At one place, the side of this rock had been blackened by campfires. Indians, trappers, prospectors, boatmen, including Bus Hatch,

Zee Grant, and perhaps Hindman, had added to this layer of soot. This was the place for my campfire.

I brought my duffle bag to this spot and then changed from wet into dry clothes, which included a heavy wool sweater and a watch cap. I was following my First Law, which is: Put on your warmest clothes first thing after getting into camp. Then I took my ax and gathered quantities of firewood. In Maine, I had been taught to start a fire with the wood of a fir tree that was dead but still standing, and then to switch to birch, which burns slowly but produces a lot of heat. Here, the wood was all from conifers, softwood that consumed quickly. The trick was to build a sizeable fire that would burn down to a good set of coals. A large fire, in addition to giving me warmth, was essential for drying out my life jacket. I had plowed through waves all day, and the kapok filling of the jacket was soaked. It had no protective plastic inner lining; that was a later innovation. Restoring the buoyancy of the life jacket was important for my survival.

I had a good dinner, identical to my previous evening's. I climbed into my sleeping bag, feeling warm and comfortable. The fire was banked up against the slab of rock, near enough to throw some heat on my face. For a while, the roar of the waterfall kept me awake, but at length I dropped off to sleep.

At the same time that I was dropping off to sleep, listening to the roar of the river, Ed was trying to sleep, listening to the rumble of the wheels of the Challenger, Union Pacific's crack streamliner. He was on his way back to New York. When I didn't show up for supper on the previous evening, Ed asked Slim to drive him back to Sun Valley. There, Ed sent off a telegram to my parents, explaining what I had done. He also had a rather gloomy interview with Taylor Williams and the Sun Valley publicity director, who sent off, by the wire service, a lurid story to the eastern papers. The story began, "Yale student feared lost in Idaho wilderness." When Ed got back to New York, he went up to New Haven to see my parents, and when they heard his account, they became quite anxious for my safety. But of all this, I was completely oblivious.

As at my first campground, I awoke cold and stiff in the morning. I could see that the sun was beginning to work its way down the western wall of the canyon, so I got out of my sleeping bag and climbed about two hundred feet up the steep slope until I was in the sunlight. This was a good spot, not only to pick up a little warmth, but also to enjoy the scenery and to do some thinking about my situation.

The canyon was a steep-sided vee, with slopes of broken rock and areas of thin soil to which pine and spruce clung with difficulty. There were many downed logs scattered on the slopes, showing that this was a battleground, the trees trying to hold on with their roots, and the forces of erosion and wind knocking them down. Some trees came out of the canyon wall almost horizontally and then turned upward, indicating that the soil had slipped since those trees were saplings. At many places, the trees had lost out completely, and broken slide rock extended from high up down to the water's edge. Pinnacles of rock and rugged cliffs added further variety. The canyon was a rough gouge, cut into the crust of the earth by the river, which boiled and twisted between steep walls at the canyon bottom. I thought of the tune "Idaho," which I had last heard from the jukebox in the tavern in Stanley. This was certainly a "yawning canyon," and it was greeting the sun.

I looked down at the grove of trees where I was camped. I knew I'd soon be down there and before I was, I had best make a decision. Should I or shouldn't I continue down the river? My plan had been to catch up to Hindman, but I had been too slow. With his knowledge of the river, he could move much faster than I could. With an early start the previous morning, he had probably reached Dagger Falls in one day, a full day ahead of me. There was no way for me to catch up, except possibly on the middle portion of the river, from Pistol Creek to Crandall Ranch. I knew from my experience on the Allegash River in

Maine that if you have a strong current but few big rapids, then it's easy to cover thirty-five miles a day. But if I could do that, so could Hindman. Catching up to him before the Impassable Canyon was only the remotest possibility, not to be counted on.

There were plenty of good reasons for calling it quits here at the falls and walking back to Cape Horn. I fully appreciated that running whitewater alone was dangerous business; in case of upset, there was no chance of rescue other than self-rescue. That was true of any river, but the Middle Fork, at least the part that I'd seen and at this stage of water, surged along with a continuous strong current. There were no calm sections between rapids where a boater, having upset, could swim his boat into shore. I also appreciated that the Middle Fork was much more difficult than any river I had previously run, not excepting the Rapid River in Maine. Between Marsh Creek and Dagger Falls, I had had several close calls. From what Zee had told me and from studying the river profile sheets, I knew that there were twenty more miles of steep river before Pistol Creek. There were even some bad spots between Pistol Creek and Crandall Ranch. After that, there were big rapids all the way to the confluence with the Main Salmon. The water level was high, much higher than when Zee had run it. I had a reprint of an article he had written about his trip. The photographs showed a stream entirely different from the river I was experiencing. I might be running the river at a stage never before attempted, except of course by Hindman, somewhere ahead of me.

Added to all those external reasons for stopping, there were the internal, personal ones: For the past two days, I had been cold, wet, and frightened most of the time. My degree of fear or anxiety or whatever it should be called wasn't enough to impair my ability to handle my boat. Perhaps it was an advantage; perhaps the added adrenaline gave me an edge in whitewater, but I was under a stress that was as palpable as the cold water that soaked me when I smashed through a standing wave.

Those were the arguments for calling it quits, and if I was to do so, this was a good place to stop. I could fold up the boat, cache it some place, then take my duffle bag and hike out to Cape Horn. I could arrange for Slim to pick up my boat later in the summer while he was on one of his pack trips along the river. If I survived the war, perhaps I could come back for another try, at a better season and with two or three companions.

Against this formidable array in favor of stopping, there were only a few arguments in favor of going on. So far, I was making it. My skill was increasing with every mile. I was compensating for the danger of running alone by being particularly careful, scouting each rapid, picking conservative routes. More important, to run the Middle Fork had been a consuming ambition, almost a passion. Now that I had ridden Marsh Creek and the river down a thousand feet of altitude, each foot hard fought, it was difficult to give up, to admit defeat. I was well into the canyon, and it was intolerable not to see what was downstream, not to experience the rest of this wilderness, not to pass through the Impassable Canyon. Added to those arguments, the sun was out; it was a beautiful day to be running a river.

That was my self-examination, my coming to terms with my own folly. It was like Jack pausing one-third of the way up the beanstalk to consider whether it might not be more prudent to climb down, or St. George wondering if the princess was adequate compensation for facing the dragon. Such doubts have only one answer. I decided to keep going.

5

Dangerous Water

The decision made, I went down the slope, gathering an armful of wood on the way. I built a good fire and cooked breakfast, the same as the day before. I was by now quite adept at tossing pancakes; I had dropped only one in the fire. When breakfast was over, I carried my boat down the steep bank to the river and tied in my duffle bag. There was a rapid just below the put-in place; Zee would have called it a tail twister. I scouted it briefly, went back to the boat, climbed in, and shoved off.

Between the falls and Sulfur Creek there were a couple of bad spots, but by careful scouting I got through them. I could see that this was going to be another slow day, with more time spent on shore than on the river. Stopping at the hot springs would further reduce the number of miles I could expect to cover that day, but I was no longer in a race to catch Hindman, and a hot soak would do me good. Also, I wanted to try fishing the creek. Slim said that at this season the side creeks sometimes yielded more fish than the river.

The rapid just above the creek had more rocks showing than most. I ran it on a diagonal course and swung into shore at the creek mouth.

I took my fly rod and hiked upstream along the bank of the creek. Sulfur Creek was much smaller than either Marsh or Bear Valley Creek. The banks were very bushy, but I was able to follow game trails. After a mile of following the creek, I came to a clearing in which there was a log cabin. As I stepped into the clearing on one side, a deer disappeared into the forest on the other. There was no one in or near the cabin, no footprints, trampled grass, or any other indication that the place had been recently occupied.

In the course of exploring the clearing, I came across a hot spring. It was close to the creek: Very convenient, I thought, to have hot and cold water side by side. The spring was a depression in the ground, about eight feet across and four feet deep. It had been lined with rocks. I tested the water: hot but not excessively so, and with a faint smell of sulfur. I took off my clothes and was soon in the relaxing water. How great to be soaking in a natural hot tub, open to a beautiful blue sky, in a forest clearing, and at least twenty miles from the nearest other human being.

As I looked about me, I suddenly noticed that a snake was curled around one of the rocks on the far side of the pool. The snake was part in and part out of the water. I could see neither its head nor its tail and had no clue as to whether it was a rattlesnake or some harmless water snake. Whichever, the snake had prior claim to the pool. I got out and walked across the meadow toward the cabin, enjoying the cool air on my skin.

The log cabin was of unusual design. It consisted of two square cabins with a covered breezeway between. Both cabins had doors opening onto the breezeway. One door, which apparently led to the living quarters, was closed and locked with a rusty padlock. The opposite door stood slightly ajar. The door creaked when I pushed it open, revealing another hot spring which took up the entire inside of the cabin. This cabin had no windows, so it was quite dark inside. I held open the door and studied the pool to be sure there were no occupants. Seeing none, I entered, let the door close behind me, and slipped into the pool. Except for light filtering through cracks between the logs, it was very dark. With no breeze to carry away the fumes, the smell of sulfur was strong. I soaked for a half-hour, wondering if the people who had lived here had abandoned the place permanently and wondering what their life had been like. Their days may have been full of hard work, but in the evenings they had the luxury of hot baths.

I climbed out of the pool and stepped through the door into the sunlight, which seemed overbright to my dark-adapted eyes. When the sun and the air had dried me, I dressed and went down to the creek to see if I could catch any fish. I flicked a wet royal coachman downstream and worked it among the rocks. A strike, and I quickly landed a nine-inch trout. It was silvery with dark spots, like a rainbow trout but with red streaks on the lower jaw. From this I knew it to be a cutthroat trout, the first of that species that I had ever caught. I moved downstream, casting among the rocks of the creek, but there were no more strikes. The sun was climbing in the sky; I knew that I must be on my way and would have to be content with only one fish to supplement my standard diet. Back at the boat, I stowed my fishing rod, put on my soggy life jacket, and set out once again on the river.

Shortly after leaving Sulfur Creek, I saw a badger digging in gravel about fifteen feet up the left bank. My job the previous summer had been with a man who made movies of wild animals. I suspect the technique is still used today: We let animals out of cages to simulate wild situations. I was familiar with badgers and knew that the hiss was part of their language, so I hissed at the animal. He snapped his head around as if some other badger had called his name. He saw me but didn't seem at all alarmed. He went back to his digging and I drifted on.

I now realized that I was on flat water; there was a current, but very little drop. The river was growing wider, and dead trees stuck up through the water along both banks. I drifted around a bend and discovered the reason for the river's change of character. An enormous volume of broken rock filled the bottom of the canyon. Scars on the canyon walls indicated the origin of at least some of this material, though some may have been swept into the river from side creeks. This cataclysmic event could not have happened many years earlier because bark and dead pine needles still clung to the trees that stuck out of the impounded water. This mass of broken rock formed a natural dam, through which the river had punched its own spillway. From my seat in the foldboat, I could see only the lip of the spillway, but I could hear the roar of the water as it went down the far side. I pulled over to the right bank so as not to be sucked into the chute, and I found a landing place against the upstream side of the dam. Here silt and small rocks had accumulated against the blocks of raw granite, piled in confusion, that formed the bulk of the rock slide. In the silt were footprints, some like the print I had seen back at the falls. There was also an impression that could have been made by the bottom of a boat, pulled up on shore. Hindman was surely ahead of me; he had stopped to look over this same place.

I stood on the bank and looked, almost in disbelief, at the chute. In a hundred yards, the river made up all of the normal drop for the past quarter-mile of flat water. There were waves everywhere, sharp, frothy waves that seemed to have no pattern. Near the bottom, in dead center, there was a logjam. This place was a greater challenge than anything I'd come through so far. It was far above my ability level. It must have been the spot where Zee upset, losing his river maps and damaging his movie camera. That had been at much lower water, when rocks were showing. Now there were no rocks, only a tumult of waves.

The first thing I considered was to carry my boat and duffle around the chute. I examined the rock slide to see if there was any reasonable way of getting over it. There was none. The fragments of the canyon wall lay heaped just as if the slide had occurred the day before. Certainly, I could carry the boat over this mass of rocks, but it would be hard work with the chance of slipping and breaking a leg. For the past forty-eight hours I'd been wet and cold a good percentage of the time. The hot spring had been a help, but I was beginning to feel a bit weak. The carry would take at least an hour, perhaps two, and I'd have to camp far short of the ten or twelve miles I'd allotted myself for the day.

Once again I considered quitting altogether. It seemed a shame, though, to give up without a try at the chute. If I should run it and upset, the worst that could happen to me, short of drowning, would be to lose my boat and all my duffle. If that happened, I could still hike out. I could make my way to Sulfur Creek and spend the night in the shelter over the hot spring. It might not be the height of comfort, but I'd be warm. The next day, I could hike the twenty miles to Cape Horn. This seemed a reasonable contingency plan; I decided to run the chute.

I concentrated on studying the confusion of waves, and, as always happens, the features of the rapid began to sort themselves out. I picked a route, establishing checkpoints that avoided as many waves as possible in the upper portion of the chute. Some haystacks, as big waves are often called, were not to be avoided, particularly at the bottom where I could see a curl of white that I would have to punch through, staying well to the right of the logjam. I took another long look at the chute, determined where I should drop over the lip, and memorized just how far I should be out from the right bank at various points down the long incline.

It is always difficult to translate a route, picked from the bank, into what you actually see when you're in the boat. The worst situation is when you're coming up to a drop that you can't see over. You have to judge how far you are from the bank and look ahead for some minor differences as the water accelerates and dips out of sight. As I drifted toward the chute, I was probably well lined up, but just before the lip I thought I was headed for a trouble spot and I paddled farther out in the current and went over the lip too far to the left. I was off course for the upper third of the chute, plowing through waves I had hoped to avoid. It was a wild ride, very fast. Halfway down, I was back on course, running close to the right bank. At the end, with the big waves approaching, I picked out the most likely spot and smashed through to quieter water. I was completely soaked, and there was a dangerous amount of water inside the boat, making it unstable. Very carefully, I eased into an eddy and grabbed a rock on the bank. I was elated. If I could run that chute, I could run anything. I could run "the Mill-tails of Hell."

The rapid that I had just come though was the result of a flash flood in the year 1936. Rocks and tree trunks were swept down Sulfur Creek and other tributaries and also slid directly into the river from the canyon walls. Today, the natural dam is covered by trees and brush and so is not the scene of desolation that it was in 1942. The rapid, which is called Sulfur Slide, has changed through the process of erosion. The channel is wider and less steep, and there is less of an impoundment of water above the dam. Boatmen still land above the drop to look it over and to chart their ways through. Forty years later, it is still a formidable obstacle.

I emptied the water out of the boat and was off as soon as possible. Rounding the next bend of the river, I came upon a herd of a dozen mule deer at the edge of the water. They were all does, though perhaps there were a few spike-horn bucks, but there were no mature bucks with big racks. The animals looked at me with curiosity but with no sign of fear as I slid past, very close to them. A man in a kayak was just a strange shape, no particular threat.

The river grew steeper, and I went back to my practice of stopping frequently and working my way down the bank to see what was ahead. As with the section above the falls, the process was difficult because the banks were steep and rocky and there were few eddies along the shore. Less than two miles after Sulfur Slide, I was swept past the stopping place that I had chosen, and found myself running difficult drops that I hadn't scouted. I was anxiously searching for an eddy, when up ahead I saw a sharp drop with foaming white beyond. At first I thought I was headed for a great boulder with water pouring over its top. In that case, there should be a route to one side or the other. As I came closer, I saw that the drop extended across the river. I was approaching the edge of a falls. There was no escape route. Below the falls, a great curler of a wave rolled back upstream. There was only one thing to do: I paddled ahead as hard as I could, hoping for enough momentum to carry me over the reversal.

I went over the edge. The bow bridged onto the wave. The stern dropped. The boat stopped its forward travel and started to slip back, bow in air, wavering. I paddled desperately, lunging forward and driving the paddle down as far as I could reach until the blade caught forward-moving water. With this as an anchor point, I pulled the boat up and over the wave and onto the safe water beyond.

I found an eddy and landed. As soon as my heart stopped pounding, I got out my river maps. I hadn't remembered that there was a falls in this section of river, but there it was on the map, the notation "falls," right where Velvet Creek came into the river. Then I located the same spot on the profile sheet. There was a steep section; that was where I had been swept past my landing spot. Then there was a vertical step, the falls itself.

The drop is now known as Velvet Falls, and boatmen treat it

with respect. The same configuration of the river and perhaps the same lack of caution that got me into trouble have caused many upsets and several drownings. I was fortunate that I wasn't the first. It is possible to avoid the steepest part of the drop by running close to the left bank, but by coming on the falls suddenly, I didn't see that route.

The step on my profile sheet indicated a drop of six to eight feet. I was running the river at a high enough stage to reduce this drop to about four feet, but the vertical drop wasn't the dangerous feature. The hazard came from the reversal wave,

the water boiling back upstream just below the falls. When water goes over a falls, it picks up velocity in the drop and then rushes along the streambed. The river cannot maintain this velocity for long because downstream from the falls the streambed resumes its normal, less precipitous, rate of fall. Of necessity, the slower-moving water is deeper than the swift water because the same volume of water per second must pass both points. The water must go from swift and shallow just below the falls to slow and deep farther downstream. If the streambed remains relatively flat, then this change in depth must occur through a rise in the level of the surface. This happens suddenly, at a point of balancing forces. It is an abrupt and turbulent step, known technically as a "hydraulic jump."

The hydraulic jump at Velvet Falls was a curling wave, close enough to the drop for me to bridge over to it with my boat, but between the falls and the wave was a space filled with foam, a sort of watery pit. If my boat had slid back into this pit, the boat would have swung broadside to the current and then would have rolled like a spindle between the falls and the wave. What would have happened to me is easy to imagine.

My map showed me that I was six and a half miles from Soldier Creek, and my profile sheet showed me that most of this was at thirty to forty feet per mile. After what I'd been through, that didn't seem very threatening. However, the last mile before the creek had a sixty-foot drop. Zee had warned me of a bad rapid at that place and had advised me to stop at an old mining shack that was perched above the river on the right bank. The map showed that as the river approached this place, it swung through a series of wide bends and then faced a particularly high portion of the canyon wall, towering twenty-five hundred feet above the river. With these features in mind, I pushed off again and headed downriver.

Although the river was less steep, the volume of water increased with each creek that emptied into the river. Whenever I passed one of these tributary creeks, I looked at it glumly, knowing that it brought nothing but trouble. Still, this stretch was something of a relief. I could see farther ahead and for the most part was able to pick out my route from the boat. I did come upon another landslide rapid. I had to scout that, though running this drop was much easier than running Sulfur Slide. My confidence level was up, and I was doing a better job of boat handling. Another thing to my advantage was that the air was warmer than it had been for the past two days. Perhaps that was due to the lower altitude or perhaps to a change in the weather. Whatever the cause, the warmer air was welcome because I was beginning to shiver slightly whenever I stopped paddling.

Toward the end of the afternoon, I found myself in steepening water and rounding a bend to the right. Ahead was a high cliff. Then I spotted a small log structure, perched on the right bank. I knew that if I continued around the bend, I would be swept into the rapid that Zee considered the worst in the upper river. I swung into an eddy and up to the bank, then sat for a moment considering what to do.

I had come only twelve miles since leaving Dagger Falls but had dropped a respectable four hundred and sixty feet in altitude. I had run rapids that I had not thought myself capable of handling. If there was worse to come, I would face it after a night's sleep.

6

Giving It Ten

I pulled my boat well up the bank and took the usual precaution of securing it to a tree. I didn't want to lose the boat to a sudden rise in water level caused by a cloudburst. Then I shouldered the duffle bag and climbed the bank. As I pushed through the undergrowth, I came face to face with a mule deer on its way down to the river for a drink. The animal turned and bounded up the bank ahead of me.

I found myself in an abandoned mining camp. The shack overhanging the river housed rusted machinery that was a mystery to me at the time but which I now know was a stamp mill, used to crush gold-bearing rock. The mill had been powered by a waterwheel, and for that reason, the rapid starting at this point has been called Waterwheel Rapid or, more often, Powerhouse Rapid.

A light rain was beginning to fall, and I was anxious to find a sheltered spot for my sleeping bag. A short distance from the stamp mill there was a cabin, its door missing and its roof two-thirds gone. There was some protection near the east wall, and I decided to sleep there. I changed to dry clothes and then looked for a place to build a fire, preferably out of the wind, which was now beginning to blow. I couldn't find a good place outside the cabin. Inside, in the center of the dirt floor seemed the best choice. The fire would be protected from the wind, and the smoke would escape through the mostly open roof. There was an ancient broom in one corner of the cabin. I used it to sweep the floor. Then I brought in stones and built a small hearth for my fire. My dinner that evening was the same that I had eaten the previous two evenings except that it was augmented by the trout I had caught in Sulfur Creek. I did well enough eating with my fingers and my knife to wonder why people had invented forks and spoons.

As I ate my supper, I thought about the miners who had lived in the cabin and about the Indians who had lived in the area at a not very distant time. How difficult life must have been for them. They faced life-and-death decisions all the time. Most people living in a civilized setting go for years without facing such a choice. For people living in the wilderness, such choices are commonplace. In running the Middle Fork, I was receiving an introduction to the unprotected way of life. The decision of how to run a rapid, or even when and where to camp, was more important to my survival than any decisions I had ever made.

That night I was warmer than I had been the past two nights. The only problem was that there were more pack rats than usual. As I was dropping off to sleep, I heard them scurrying around and once or twice felt them running across my sleeping bag. In the morning I discovered that they had chewed a small hole in my life jacket and pulled out some of the kapok filling, not enough to pose a threat, but enough to annoy me. While I was cooking breakfast, a pack rat jumped through the door, landing on the other side of the fire from me. He turned and left the way he had come in.

After breakfast, I scouted downriver for three-quarters of a mile. The slope was not very steep but was forested, the trees and undergrowth extending to the edge of a forty-foot cliff that dropped down into the surging waters of the river. I found it difficult to get more than a small view of the river from any one spot on the top of the cliff, but by looking down from several vantage points, I was able to piece together the general configuration of the rapid.

I went back to the mining camp, loaded my boat, and shoved off. At the starting point, the river was quite steep, with a fast current kicking up standing waves in midstream. As I was on the inside of the bend, I was in slower-moving water. I hugged the right bank among rocks that acted as a brake to the current. Here I struck an underwater rock, one of only two that I hit in the entire length of the Middle Fork. I judged from the impact that there would be no more than a minor scrape on the rubberized canvas hull. This game of sticking close to the right bank had to end, for downstream on the right was the cliff, with the full force of the river charging into it as the river came out of its right turn and angled left. There was a break in the turbulence in midstream, not a real slowing of the current, but enough calm so I could drive diagonally across the river. As I had hugged the right, now I hugged the left bank, glad to be out of the main current with its big waves and growling souse holes, those foaming pits in the river that can swallow up the unwary boater. Finally, where the current churned into the angle of the overhanging cliff, I slid over a gravel bar far on the left and well out of danger.

It was a long rapid, but I had come through according to plan and relatively easily. Zee had run this stretch at very low water, when the channel was much restricted, and he was obliged to maneuver in the boulder-filled center of the river. At the end, he must have been forced almost against the cliff. The sneak routes, which were available to me, were for him high and dry on the bank. This was an instance in which high water made a rapid easier.

After this good beginning, the day went poorly for me. My problem was less with the river than with the weather, which had deteriorated since the day before. Sometimes the sun shone, but more often it was hidden by clouds that swept by just over the tops of the surrounding hills. Cold winds, rain, and sleet spilled into the canyon, making me miserable. I had a poncho of rubberized cloth, but to wear it would have made paddling awkward and could have entangled me in an upset. So I let the rain and sleet soak me; after all, I was already soaked by the river. Every time I punched through a wave, some of the water slid along the spray deck and poured down into the small open cockpit and down onto my stomach and thighs. Larger waves would drench my face and my upper body. The river water was very cold, as much of it came from melting snow high in the mountains. My chill, which had started the day before, came back, and whenever I stopped paddling, I shook involuntarily. To reduce this shivering, I drove the boat downriver most of the time, without scouting rapids that I would have looked over the day before. When I absolutely had to scout a drop, I did it as quickly as possible.

By the time I reached Rapid River, a big tributary that came in from the right, the chill was severe. I considered stopping for the night but thought I would probably be cold again the next day and in worse shape. Both Zee and Slim had told me that a few people lived along the middle portion of the river. There was a Forest Service ranger station near Indian Creek. Slim's friend, Milt Hood, had a cabin about five miles beyond Marble Creek. At either place, I'd find shelter for the night. I'd be warm, get over my chills, and be able to continue on downriver. Meanwhile, I had to keep moving.

A mile past Rapid River, I found myself floating on another

stretch of flat water. There were dead trees sticking out of the water near the bank and a great scar on the canyon wall where rock had broken away and cascaded to the bottom of the canyon. I knew that up ahead there was another dam caused by a landslide. As I paddled on the flat water, I imagined the riverbed dropping away below me at a steady forty feet per mile. I was going into debt to the river. All of that drop of streambed would have to be paid back in one whoosh.

When I reached the landslide rock dam, I paddled up to the shore on the left where there was a small beach of silt between two dead trees. Here again were Hindman's footprints. I seemed to be in agreement with him as to where to land above a bad place.

As soon as I stopped paddling, I started to shiver, and when I got out of the boat, the shivering grew worse. I hurried over the broken slabs to a place where I could look at the spillway. I could see that it was a long, straight incline, with very fast water rushing down it, and big standing waves heaping up for the full length of the chute. I supposed that it was runnable, perhaps no worse than the first landslide rapid I'd run the day before, but before I could commit myself to this piece of whitewater, I'd have to pick a good course. While I was shivering, I found it impossible to do an adequate job of studying the rapid.

So long as I had been paddling, my muscular activity had produced just enough body heat to keep up my body temperature. Now that I had stopped paddling, my body was trying to produce the same heat through the involuntary muscular activity of shivering. This was the beginning of hypothermia, a very dangerous condition in which body temperature gets progressively lower. One of the by-products of hypothermia is the deterioration of the power of judgment. The end point of hypothermia is death.

I didn't know anything about hypothermia, but I knew I was in a trap. Continued paddling had kept me from shivering. I couldn't keep paddling because I first had to pick a course down the chute. I couldn't pick a course down the chute because I was shivering. I realized that the way out of the trap was to have another source of heat. I would build a fire.

The cold wind in my face, I stumbled back to the boat, got out my ax, and started looking for dry wood. The two dead trees near my landing place had long since lost their bark, and the gray wood was soaked by rain. I was on the same side of the river that had been scoured by the landslide, so there was very little standing vegetation nearby, and all of it was wet. The trap was becoming complicated and more serious. I considered climbing back into my boat and paddling upstream. In the flat section I could make headway against the current and perhaps cross over to the other side and find dry wood and a place to build a fire. I rejected that idea because I needed my fire here, at the head of the chute, so I could warm myself and then, without delay, pick my course.

My teeth chattering and all my body shaking, I searched the top of the slide for driftwood. I found a few pieces small enough to carry and hacked a couple of branches off a log. This activity momentarily calmed my shaking. I carried and dragged the wood back toward the boat. I piled up the wood hastily and then looked in my duffle bag for paper. I found my maps, but they were too precious to burn. I also had a reprint of an article written by Zee about his Middle Fork trip, a partial roll of toilet paper, and a paperback copy of Agatha Christie's *Murder in the Calais Coach*. Why I had taken that along, I don't know, but it was obviously the most expendable item. Unfortunately, it wouldn't burn; neither would Zee's article.

In my desperation, I had done a poor job of preparing my fire. It is possible to start a fire under almost any condition, but you have to go about it properly. I knew that even though I was shaking terribly, I must begin again and build my fire methodically.

I took the spray deck from the boat and wedged it against one of the trees. That was to provide a screen against the wind and the rain. I arranged a few rocks as a hearth, piled my wood close by, and tried to cut slivers of wood with my knife. This was difficult because of my shaking hands, and I found I could do a better job with my ax. With these slivers and with a few twigs, I attempted to build a tepee of wood around a crumpled piece of toilet paper, but my hands would not work well enough to place the slivers and twigs where they belonged.

What I needed to break out of the trap was just enough control of my hands to get the fire going. One bit of sunlight would be sufficient. I looked up at the sky. The cloud cover, just above the canyon rim and moving rapidly, wasn't continuous; there were a few breaks through which I had glimpses of blue sky. If only one of those gaps in the clouds would move between me and the sun.

The trap I was in was so complete that I felt it wasn't just a chance combination of circumstances, but a design, either to test me or to destroy me. I felt, perhaps irrationally, that I was facing a good deal more than the problem of building a fire and running a rapid. In school and college, my interests had been in mathematics and science, and if I had felt the tug of another reality, it was from reading poetry and drama. Several years before, I had read Marlowe's *Dr. Faustus* and it had made a deep impression on me. Faustus had bargained his soul away in return for riches and power. Shivering, and in desperate trouble on the banks of the Middle Fork, would I go so far for a minute of sunlight?

As those thoughts flashed through my mind, an opening in the clouds did come between me and the sun. I felt the warmth on my face and held up my hands to receive as much light as possible. My shivering stopped. Working quickly and efficiently, I arranged my twigs and slivers of wood, struck a match, lit the bottom of the pyramid, and built up the fire, using progressively larger pieces of wood. When the fire was at its peak, I got as close to it as I could, soaking up the heat.

When I felt I had a few minutes' reserve, I hurried across the slide to the edge of the chute.

The chute, I could see, was very turbulent, but most of the waves were in the center. Diagonal waves were thrown out by rocks protruding from the side, but the waves weren't particularly high until they met in the center. The left edge of the chute, close to the bank, was a reasonable route all the way to the bottom where there were the usual large standing waves as the chute emptied into slower water.

I hurried back to the fire, soaked up a little more heat, then repacked the boat and replaced the spray deck. Deprived of the spray deck's protection, the fire was all but put out by the rain, but I tossed the few still-smoldering sticks into the river. Then I eased the boat into the water, climbed into the cockpit, paddled a short distance upstream, turned and carefully lined the boat up with the left edge of the lip at the top of the chute.

Once in the chute, I discovered that there was a crosscurrent tending to push me toward the center. There must have been a corresponding current on the other side. The friction of the water on the sides and bottom of the chute caused the water to flow in a great double vortex, turning clockwise on my side of the river and counterclockwise on the other. To counteract this force, I paddled forward only with my right paddle blade, and so kept close to the left bank. I went down the chute very fast and at the bottom slid between standing waves on my right and an eddy on my left. I had come through without shipping any water. More important, my chill was gone; I felt stronger and that I had been given a reprieve.

Pistol Creek was no more than two miles ahead. I pushed on eagerly because Zee had told me that the creek marked the boundary between the steep upper river and the less difficult middle section. I was too eager, not cautious enough about stopping and scouting ahead, and so the next emergency burst on me entirely in contrast to the slow development of my problem at the chute.

I came to a place where a trail bridge crossed the river. The channel narrowed and dropped between steep rocky banks that blocked a view of what was downstream. Ahead was a sharp turn to the left and an obviously accelerating current. I looked for an eddy in which to land but could find none. When I was well into the throat of the narrow section and could look around the corner to the left, I saw that the river made an abrupt turn to the right immediately after the left turn and, at the same time, it dropped sharply. In the middle of the drop, stretching across the channel, was a log. The current was carrying me toward the log at breakneck speed. The log was too low to slip under; at places it skimmed the top of the water. If I should hit the log, I would be spilled into the water with a smashed boat.

Immediately after seeing the log, I spotted an eddy, a pocket against the right bank and just big enough for the boat. I drove to the right and plunged the bow of the boat into the eddy. The pull of the current was too strong; the boat swung around, stern dropping into a long suck that led down to the log. The bow began to slip out of the eddy. I found myself paddling uphill, using every ounce of strength I possessed. At Yale I had rowed on the lightweight varsity crew and so knew the value of "giving it ten." In this most serious race, with ten strong strokes and then ten more I pulled the boat up into the safety of the eddy.

There seemed no alternative but to carry around the drop, but in climbing along the bank, I discovered another route. This rapid was typical of rapids formed by resistant bedrock. The river, in cutting through the rock, had formed a narrow, twisting channel. At the bottom, a ledge deflected the current to the left where it found a passage over and through an opening in the ledge. That was the main channel, the one blocked by the log, but to the right of that channel was a narrow cleft in the ledge, and through this there poured enough water to float my boat, though certainly nothing wider. This high-water sneak passage couldn't be entered directly from my eddy of refuge, because I'd surely be swept into the log, but by lifting the boat over the rocks at the downstream end of the eddy, I was able to slide the boat to the entrance to the passage. I positioned the boat carefully, climbed back in still holding onto the rocks, then let go my hold. I plunged down a steep drop in a narrow slot between rock walls, guiding the boat by pushing with my hands against the rock. There was no space to use the paddle. Mostly, the boat found its own way through, riding the small fraction of the river's current that took this path. At the bottom, I shot out of the slot onto the full river.

A short way downstream, Pistol Creek came in from the left, adding its load of water to the Middle Fork. The upper river was behind me. Ahead was the middle river with its drop of only twenty to thirty feet per mile. As I pushed on, I found a few tough spots, and I occasionally shipped water going through waves, but when this happened I was able to drift through the next easy stretch, holding the paddle with one hand and bailing with the other. Matching the change in the river was a change in the canyon. The upper river had been characterized by steep slopes crowding the river, slide rock, cliffs, patches of dark forest, fallen trees scattered on the slopes. Here the canyon was more open, its contours more gentle, the forest less dark.

The storm had blown over, the air seemed warmer, and as the river swung to the northeast, the afternoon sun found its way to the bottom of the canyon. On the right, a small flock of magpies, the first I had seen in the canyon, rose into the air and called raucously. I was sure that they were welcoming me to the middle river. I was glad to be there with the tensions of the upper river behind.

Still, I was not completely over my experience at the chute. From time to time, I entertained the fantasy that the canyon walls were not real, that they were mere stage scenery, put there by God, who was just on the other side, standing between the props that held the scenery up. Such thoughts worried me, as I knew I was in a situation in which I must not let my mind wander from physical reality. It was important that I find a place to spend the night. I started scanning the left bank, hoping to spot the ranger station that was somewhere in this area. At the same time, the sun dropped behind the canyon wall and the air grew cooler. Once again I had to keep paddling to avoid shivering.

I was on the point of stopping at the first likely campsite, when I looked through an opening in a stand of ponderosa pines on the left bank and saw a cabin. I had only a brief glimpse before the trees hid it from view, but I had seen the peak of a roof and, just below the peak, the skull and spreading antlers of an elk. This seemed more to me than just a decoration. The antlers were a symbol that conveyed some mystery but also extended a welcome.

7

Unexpected Visitor

As soon as I could find an eddy, I landed, pulled my boat up on the bank, and walked back to the cabin, which was located beside a small stream. As I stepped onto the porch, a cat jumped up and scurried around the side of the cabin. The door was ajar. I knocked, and after a pause a voice from just behind the door said, "Come in." I stepped inside and looked down to my right, where a man was sitting at a table, eating a plate of potatoes and beans. He was about forty years old and was short and wiry. He stared at me with an expression I found quite disconcerting. I thought it best to explain myself right off.

"I've been coming down the river in a boat, alone. I've been pretty cold most of the time. I've been getting the chills. I thought that if I could get indoors for one night, I'd be in better shape. I was trying to reach Milt Hood's place. How far is that?"

"About eight miles."

"What about the ranger? Are you the ranger?"

"No. He's back upstream, close to three miles."

"I must have gone by his place without seeing it."

"It sets back from the river," he said.

Milt Hood's was too far downstream, and I didn't want to hike back to the ranger station. This man's cabin was neat and warm; the potatoes and beans smelled delicious.

"I don't think I can make it to Milt Hood's. Can you put me up for the night, and possibly give me a meal?"

"Sure," he said, "but I can't promise you anything fancy. I've got spuds and beans, that's about all."

"Sounds fine to me," I said. "I've been eating flapjacks and ham for four days, and I'm sick of it."

I then introduced myself. He told me his name.

"Budell. Ed Budell," he said, and we shook hands.

I left my life jacket beside the stove to dry out and went down to the river to get my duffle bag. It was growing dark, and I was glad that I had stopped. When I got back to the cabin, Budell was frying more potatoes on his wood-burning stove. I went to the back of the cabin and changed into my dry clothes.

"Do you want to wash up before you eat?" Budell asked. "There's a basin outside on the porch and a bucket of cold water. Here's hot water on the stove."

I thanked him and took the kettle outside. The basin was on a shelf beside the door, and above the basin was a small mirror. I looked in the mirror and laughed. My face was streaked with soot. I had four days' worth of whiskers. My hair, never under very good control, was pointed in every direction.

"Boy!" I said. "I'm a sight. I look like a wild man."

Budell had been standing in the doorway watching me. He said, "When you're ready, come on in; supper's on the table. You're probably pretty hungry. Coming down the river alone, eh? That's something."

His voice was entirely different, more relaxed. I looked at

him and saw that he was smiling. His eyes had none of the peculiar look that I'd seen when I first stepped in the door. It occurred to me that I had frightened him, both by my sudden knock on his door and by my disheveled appearance. Budell himself was very neat, his face close shaven, hair brushed, clothes in good repair. His cabin was orderly, the porch swept clean. He was a fastidious backwoodsman, while I, about to start my senior year at Yale, was a ruffian and a tramp by comparison.

"I must have given you a start, coming through your door like that," I ventured.

"That's all right," he said. "I don't have many visitors here. Oh, I see the ranger from time to time and some of the people from downriver, but mostly I'm alone. There was a kid staying here awhile, but he got killed."

The episode at the wash basin had released Ed Budell's tongue. He talked all during the time I was eating and on into the evening. He told me that he had lived most of his life in the backcountry, in winter working as a cow hand or as a trapper, in summer panning gold or working for the Forest Service. In spite of his isolated life, he was interested in what was happening in the world. We talked about the war and he asked me why I had chosen to sign up with the marines, a question I could answer only in the vaguest terms. A few weeks before, he had gone "outside," meaning Challis or Stanley or some other place with a road, and had tried to enlist in the army.

"They wouldn't take me," he said angrily. "Said I had an incurable disease. I'm all right for ordinary work, but if you stand me over here and spin me around three times and ask me to do something, I wouldn't be able to do it right off."

"Maybe a lot of people couldn't do something right after being spun around three times," I suggested.

"That's right," said Ed. "I think I'm in as good shape as anyone, maybe better shape. I think those doctors don't know what they're talking about."

"Sure, they can make mistakes," I said, but I wondered if the doctor had been right, and if so, what the diagnosis had been. We were silent for a while, and then I added, "You say that someone was staying here but he was killed?"

"Oh, yes," said Budell. "He was a young fellow, not quite right in the head. He'd been in a lot of trouble on the outside, couldn't get along. His dad left him here with me."

"Did you have problems with him?"

"No, he was no trouble. I taught him to do some trapping, and he liked that. He did some fishing and was even able to kill his own meat. The rest of the time he hung around the cabin reading all those magazines you see back there."

"What happened to him?"

"He wanted to visit his parents in Pocatello over the Fourth of July. That's where his dad works for the railroad. The kid hiked down to Loon Creek and was planning to hike out the trail from there, but a plane had landed at the strip there on some business. The pilot offered to give the kid a ride to Boise. The plane crashed. That's how the kid was killed."

"What about the pilot?"

"He got out of it. Maybe he had a few scratches."

So that was the story of the kid. Nothing sinister, only pathetic. The magazines Budell had referred to were piled in the back of the cabin. There were westerns and romances, hundreds of them. As with all supplies and equipment, they had been hauled in from the outside over many miles of trail. Perhaps the magazines came a few at a time, but in total they were a full load for a pack horse or mule, an animal that could have carried food, or tools, or kerosene. That struck me as a curious allocation of resources.

We turned in early. I slept in the bunk recently vacated by the kid. Ed piled it high with blankets, so that I was warm that night. In spite of being warm, I slept poorly. I felt as if I were running a fever, perhaps as a result of my chills of the past few days. I lay awake for a long time, listening to the sound of the creek, rushing past the cabin. The story of the kid kept turning over in my mind. At length, I slept.

In the morning when I got up, I felt weak. "I didn't sleep too well last night," I told Ed. "I guess getting over the chills isn't that easy."

"Maybe you should stop over here a day," he suggested.

"Thanks, but I've got to push on. I've already made my train reservations to go back East."

Ed had another suggestion. "Perhaps you could go on down to Milt Hood's and spend the night there."

That sounded like a good idea. Eight miles would be a short day, but if I were in good shape the day after that, I might be able to push all the way to Crandall Ranch. Ed had a Forest Service telephone in his cabin. This ancient instrument was equipped with a hand crank that rang a bell in each of several cabins that were spaced out, miles apart, along the river. Each person in the system had a code, so many rings. Ed cranked the handle four times to signal that the call was for Milt Hood and Milt Hood only.

"Milt," Budell called into the mouthpiece, "this is Ed. There's a young fellow here, come down the river in a boat. If he shows up at your place, can you put him up for the night?"

"Let me talk to him," I suggested. Budell handed me the earpiece of the ancient instrument.

"Mr. Hood?" I said into the mouthpiece.

"Yes," came the faint answer.

"I'm coming down the river in a foldboat, a kind of kayak. Slim Hendrick suggested I stop off at your place."

"Good," came the answer. "We'll be glad to have you stop here. Spend the night."

"Thank you," I said, then added, "Mr. Hood, have you seen anything of another party going down the river?"

"They stopped by late yesterday afternoon, then kept going." he said.

"Thank you. I'll be along," I said.

So much for catching up to Hindman. He was more than a day ahead of me.

Ed had already started to cook breakfast on his wood stove. I got out my ham and cut a thick slice for each of us. While we were eating, Ed placed some pieces of rock on the table and asked if I had any idea what they were. I had taken an introductory course in geology but hadn't been exposed to enough mineralogy to make an identification.

"This looks something like feldspar," I said, "but I'm sorry I have no idea what it really is, nor what it's worth."

Budell said that he planned to take the samples to an assay office. He put the rocks away, and I brought out my maps and asked him to point out where we were. The creek beside the cabin was Pungo Creek. I had come sixteen miles the day before, a respectable distance. In four days, I had covered forty percent of the distance from Cape Horn to the junction of the Middle Fork with the Main Salmon, but I had dropped sixty percent of the altitude. I was pleased with this progress. While the map was out, I asked Ed to point out the location of Milt Hood's cabin. He did so and also warned me about a sharp drop just past Marble Creek. By now Ed was through breakfast and ready to do a day's work for the Forest Service.

"Just leave when you're ready," he suggested. "Take your time over coffee, and when you go out, snap the padlock on the door."

I thanked him for his hospitality. We shook hands.

"If you're ever this way again, stop in," he said, and left.

I sat there, thinking about this man and the solitary life he led on the banks of the Middle Fork. My preconceived notion was that a person living alone in the wilderness was likely to be rather unkempt, rough mannered, or even dangerous. Ed Budell was the opposite of that mental picture. In his personal appearance, in the orderliness of his living space, in his behavior, he was more civilized than many people I'd met in Ivy League environments. Most important, he was a kind and generous person. He gave me food and shelter when I needed it most. I felt sorry for Ed. I suspected that the doctor who had given him his army physical may have been right, and that Ed had not long to live.

I was completely wrong. Ed Budell stayed on at the Pungo Creek cabin until 1965, working for the Forest Service and trying to develop a fluorspar mine. That was the ore he had shown me, a valuable mineral, but there was not enough of it to make Ed rich. Forty years later, I discovered that he was living in Nampa, Idaho, busy making rawhide bridles and riatas, a craft for which he had become well known among Idaho cattle ranchers. It was through a chance meeting with a rancher in Challis, Idaho, that I was able to re-establish contact with Budell and through a series of letters to learn more about his life at Pungo Creek. But all that was far in the future as I sat at the table in his cabin, drinking my coffee.

When I was finished, I locked the door and started down the trail, my duffle bag on my shoulder. A mule deer, a buck with impressive antlers, was raiding Ed's small vegetable garden on the far side of his woodpile. The buck saw me and took off, bounding up the hillside in back of the cabin.

During the night the river had dropped six inches. I hoped this was a constant drop, for I wanted less water in the river when I entered the Impassable Canyon. I knew, however, that the six-inch drop might be part of a daily fluctuation. Back of the canyon walls on both sides of the river were mountains between nine and ten thousand feet high. The snow in these mountains would melt much more during the day than during the night, causing a daily rise and nightly fall in the creeks draining the mountains, and perhaps similar changes in the river itself.

Once on the river, I was glad I had stopped at Ed Budell's cabin on Pungo Creek because I soon ran into a series of pitches that would have given me trouble in the fading light of the previous afternoon. In the morning, I was able to run most of them without scouting from the bank. I would approach each drop slowly, looking ahead to see where there was the greatest danger from rocks and waves and where was the best path to avoid these problems. Then I'd paddle to whatever filament of water would lead me where I wanted to go. After that I would use as little effort as possible in sliding down the rapid. If a pitch was at a bend of the river, say a turn to the right, I would enter the fast water as close to the right bank as possible with the bow pointed diagonally across the river to the left. Rather than paddle forward, I would either drift or backpaddle to stay in the slower-moving water on the inside of the curve. The inside of the curve was likely to be shallow and rocky. If the rocks proved too much of a hazard, a few forward strokes took me as far out into the main current as I wished.

I used another lazy approach to maneuvering in the whitewater. If I entered a pitch to the left of center of the river, but decided that I should be more to the right, I would look ahead for a large rock in midstream. Beyond the rock there would be an eddy. I would pass close beside the rock and then slip the bow of the boat into the eddy, far enough beyond the rock to avoid snapping the boat around in an eddy turn, but where there was enough current differential to turn the boat about forty-five degrees without any effort on my part. Then I would paddle forward, crossing the eddy diagonally. On the far side of the eddy, the current would straighten the boat out onto its new course.

I also used eddies to slow down my progress through rapids, giving me extra time to pick a course. Again, passing close to a rock on my right, I would use a push stroke behind me on the left to drop the stern of the boat into the eddy below the rock. Once the stern was in the eddy, the bow would also swing in. I could then sit in the slack water, looking downstream to determine my course. When my mind was made up, I could move into the current, right or left.

My boat-handling technique had improved since starting

down Marsh Creek. No longer was I just sitting in the boat, trying to control it. The boat was now a part of me, as though muscle and nerve and bone extended to every portion of the hull. My paddle was equally a part of me. When not taking a stroke to propel the boat forward or back, I kept one blade or the other in contact with the water to adjust position sideways, to steer, or to stabilize.

About midday, coming through a steep pitch at a bend in the river, I turned right into a large eddy for a moment's rest. I looked down into the clear water at a confused pattern. I could see rocks on the bottom and, superimposed on the rocks, a shifting net of illumination, an irregular grid of light and dark areas caused by the refraction of sunlight by the waves on the surface of the water. At first I saw only the rocks, but suddenly, in the middle of this pattern, the outline of a fish crystallized, a large trout, almost perfectly camouflaged.

I landed the boat and got out my fishing equipment. I assembled the rod, mounted the reel, strung line and leader, and then tied on a big brown and white bucktail streamer. Then I stood on a rock at the very head of the eddy and cast into the current, letting the streamer swing into the eddy. I retrieved very slowly, letting the streamer sink, sometimes drifting and sometimes coming toward me with the slightest tension on the line. I felt a tug on the line and set the hook in a solid fish. The trout fought hard, an entirely underwater fight, but I was using fairly heavy tackle and soon brought him in. I had no landing net and so had to draw the fish close enough to slip my fingers under the gill covers and lift the fish from the water. I was holding an eighteen-inch cutthroat trout. When I had killed the fish, I debated whether or not to try another spot, since the other fish in the eddy might have been scared off by the commotion of the first fish on the end of the line. I decided to have another try at the same place. I cast my fly just as I had before. Almost immediately after it drifted into the eddy, I had another fish, this one a little smaller than the first, but still a fine fish. I repeated the process, and within half an hour had six trout, all weighing between one and two pounds. That was enough, and so I stopped. I was fishing on the opposite side of the river from the trail. It's possible that the spot had rarely if ever been fished before.

When I started downstream again, I sang. I had a variety of reasons for singing: I had come through the difficult upper river; the sun was out, and I was in no danger of a chill such as I had experienced the day before; I had set myself a goal of only eight miles that day; the rapids were a pleasure to run; I had just made a fantastic catch of trout, not even matched by some of my experiences in northern Maine. All those were contributing factors, but the chief reason I opened my mouth in song was that there was no one to hear me. I was completely alone and beyond criticism if I sang off key. Many of my friends at college sang in the glee club or in choral groups, and I well knew that whenever I tried to sing, I offended their ears. On the Middle Fork it didn't matter. The canyon walls echoed to "A capital ship for an ocean trip . . .," "As the blackbird in the spring . . .," and other lines best forgotten. The only creatures I disturbed were the magpies, and they complained stridently.

The scenery in this part of the canyon was delightful. The spot where Marble Creek came into the Middle Fork was particularly attractive. The river made a swing from a north-easterly to a southerly course. Right at the bend, Marble Creek came in from the north. Water seemed to be flowing in all directions. On the riverbanks and higher on the slopes of the canyon, scattered ponderosa pine gave the place the appearance of a carefully planned park. I stopped there for an hour, just enjoying the scene. I had heard that there were Indian drawings on the canyon walls of Marble Creek. I followed the trail beside the creek for half a mile but failed to find the petroglyphs.

Immediately after leaving Marble Creek, I could see that the river ahead of me turned to the right and went over a drop that extended in a straight line all the way across the river. Ed

Budell had warned me about this place. I landed on the right and followed a game trail downstream to have a better look. As I ducked under a pine bough, something dropped inside my collar and ran down my arm, biting me several times on the way. The creature emerged from my sleeve and dropped to the ground on a strand of silk. It was a small brown spider. Later that day my arm was stiff and sore, but there were no serious consequences of the bites.

As I had expected, the drop resembled a low falls more than an extended rapid. A slab of rock divided the channel. There was less water on the right, so I ran that side. Approaching the drop, I found myself sliding down over a gravel bar, hearing the characteristic sound of shallow water rushing over many small rocks. Ahead of me was a reverse curler, not as strong as the one at Velvet Falls but severe enough that I had to plow through it at full speed and then dig deep with my paddle to catch the forward-moving water to carry me up and over the wave.

For the next two miles, the river headed almost due south, a reversal of its general northerly direction. At the end of this stretch, on the right, lived the McCalls, who were building a small resort for fishermen. It was a reasonable place for such an enterprise because there was a small airstrip just across the river. Zee Grant and his party had stopped at the McCalls' and had supper with them, but I went by. A mile farther, just after the river turned again to head north, I slid down a long riffle and stopped on the left bank by Milt Hood's place.

As I was climbing out of the boat, a boy of about twelve and a large Newfoundland dog came running down the bank to greet me. They escorted me up the bank to where Milt Hood was waiting for me at the gate of his garden. I introduced myself and we shook hands. Milt was in his forties and he had one of the friendliest smiles I have ever encountered. His son was very like him, with the same rather long face and the same smile. Milt and his son lived in a long, low cabin. They had a large vegetable garden enclosed in a chicken-wire fence to keep out the deer. There were other buildings, including a bunkhouse. They also had a fenced pasture. The inside of the cabin showed evidence of a woman's hand—checkered oilcloth on the table, curtains in the windows—but Milt's wife was still at their winter home, in Challis, Idaho.

In the course of our conversation before supper, I learned that it was possible to use the Forest Service phone to get a message to "the outside." The telephone line ran only along the river, but the ranger had a shortwave radio transmitter. With Milt's help, I was able to send a telegram to my parents, reporting that I was halfway down the Middle Fork, that I had had no upsets, and that I would be starting through the Impassable Canyon in one more day. That must have had an ominous ring, because my parents sent a telegram to Taylor Williams, expressing their concern and asking that a lookout be kept for me.

For supper, Milt cooked my trout. There were fresh vegetables from the garden. It was a real feast. As with many people who live in isolation, Milt was starved for conversation, and we talked long into the night. Until he was sent to bed, Milt's son sat beside his father, interested in everything we had to say. The dog was always beside the boy. Milt had served in France in World War I, so we talked about the progress of the current war. It was a bad time for the Allies. In North Africa, the Germans had taken Tobruk just the week before and were now driving toward Cairo. In Russia, the Germans were hammering at Sevastopol. Milt had a battery-operated radio and had news that I was unaware of: the Japanese had landed on Kiska in the Aleutians. I told Milt that I had signed up with the marines and that I expected the war to last for twenty years. I'm sure he was thinking that if the war lasted that long, his son would be in it.

The conversation shifted to the people who went off to live in almost complete isolation in the wilderness. Milt had known many such people. He said that some were hiding from the law, and such people usually made poor company. Some lived in isolation because they had difficulty earning a living in the modern world, but in the backcountry they were able to feed themselves by hunting and fishing. Others lived in the wilderness because that was the only life they had known since childhood. All had hopes of discovering a rich vein of gold and exchanging their hardships for a life of luxury. Many frontier people were a bit crazy. Milt had stories to tell about an eccentric called Old Trapper. I asked about Earl Parrott, the hermit of the Impassable Canyon. Milt knew very little about him and had no idea whether or not he was still at his placer camp in the canyon.

"If he's still there, I'd advise staying away from him," Milt said.

I also asked Milt about the kid who had stayed with Ed Budell.

"He was a strange one," Milt said. "I think his parents had him back here so the law wouldn't find him. At one time he tried to rape an eighty-year-old woman. Well, he's dead now and no trouble to anyone."

After much more conversation, I said good night and went out to the bunkhouse. I slept soundly and awoke feeling that I had completely recovered from the chills I had experienced on the upper river.

After breakfast, Milt cranked the Forest Service telephone and talked to Frank Allison, whose cabin was fifteen miles downstream at the mouth of Loon Creek. The result of this call was an invitation for me to stop and have lunch with Frank. With regret, I said good-by to Milt and his son. They came down to the bank to see me off, the boy and the dog moving as one creature. I tied in my duffle bag, settled in the cockpit, waved, and once again was floating on the river.

8

Beyond Normal Hazard

All morning I pushed downstream, determined to make up for my slow progress of the past day. My plan was to stop at Frank Allison's for lunch and then go on to Crandall Ranch by nightfall. That was a total of thirty-two miles, but I knew I could do it. I paddled steadily, keeping the boat in the swiftest portion of the current except at places where the waves were too high, and then I would ride the side of the wave train, well on the swift-water side of the eddy line. I built up a rhythm, keeping my paddle strokes long and efficient. The boat tracked well, and it pleased me that the banks slipped by so quickly. The only thing that delayed me was my own stupidity. After I had paddled for an hour, I landed to stretch my legs. I took off my life jacket, walked around a bit, enjoying the canyon, then climbed back into the boat and shoved off. After I'd gone a mile, I realized that I wasn't wearing a life jacket. There was no alternative; I landed and walked back upstream. Fortunately, I didn't have to cross any difficult slide-rock areas nor did I have to deal with any steep cliffs coming down into the water. I found the life jacket lying close to the shore, just where I'd left it. I picked it up and hiked back downstream.

Because of this delay, it was past noon when I reached Loon Creek. This creek, which came in from the right, was one of the largest tributaries of the Middle Fork, and the trail beside the creek was a major pack route in to the river. There was a landing strip on a bench just north of the creek and beside the river. With trail, river, and landing strip, the place could have been called a transportation center.

It was by way of Loon Creek that white men first came to the canyon of the Middle Fork. In 1869 prospectors from Stanley discovered gold in the high country drained by Loon Creek. There followed a small gold rush to that area of the mountains. As was often the case, the first miners were followed by Chinese, who industriously worked over the tailings left by the first arrivals. The Chinese were not popular with the other miners and were often the victims of violence. In 1879 five Chinese were killed at Oro Grande, a mining camp on Loon Creek. Local white miners blamed Indians for the deed, but whether or not they were responsible for the deaths is open to question. The Indians of the Middle Fork area were known as the Sheepeaters. They lived entirely by hunting and gathering and were experts in the curing of hides and the making of handsome fur robes. There were never very many of these Indians, but as long as they occupied the canyons of the river, and the high country to the west of the river, miners and settlers would not penetrate into those areas. An Indian war was the obvious "final solution." Responding to local pressure, the army set itself to the task of rounding up the Sheepeaters. Just sixty-three years and two days before I stood at the mouth of Loon Creek, a small detachment of cavalry, led by Captain Reuben F. Bernard, arrived at the same spot. This was the first recorded penetration of white men into the canyon of the Middle Fork. Finding no Indians, Captain Bernard and his men moved upriver for nearly forty miles before climbing out of the canyon. They had great difficulty with their mounts and pack animals on the steep slopes of the canyon. Captain Bernard later declared the country the most rugged he had ever crossed.

The cavalry detachment then circled through the headwaters of the Middle Fork. For months, these and other soldiers wandered through the mountains of central Idaho, looking for Indians. Eventually, there was a skirmish beside Big Creek, another tributary of the Middle Fork. One soldier was killed. The troopers were fortunate enough to capture the supplies that the Indians were counting on to see them through the winter. Near a small creek the soldiers also captured an Indian woman and her baby. The woman was sent off to persuade her tribe to surrender. The baby, held hostage, cried all night. The woman came back the next morning, not having accomplished her mission. The weary soldiers returned the baby and named the creek Papoose Creek. Within a week, the Indians, a small band with very few weapons, did surrender. They were packed off to a reservation on a dry, flat plain where they were expected to live as farmers. So closed the Sheepeater Indian War, opening the Middle Fork to miners, trappers, ranchers, and in time to whitewater boaters.

I hiked up to Frank Allison's place, which was perched above the creek with a nice view across the river. Beside the cabin was a well-kept garden. I knocked on the door and was greeted by a man of advanced years, though how old he was, I couldn't guess. His head was covered by a shock of snow-white hair. He was short, but seemed shorter because of a permanent stoop. He put me at my ease at once, saying he hadn't been sure I'd show up, but just in case, he'd gone down to the creek and caught some trout. His fishing rod was leaning against the table, a delicate split bamboo, the instrument of an expert fly fisherman. I made some admiring comment.

"Good, but not so good as one I was promised but didn't get."

Without explaining his statement, he pointed to a chair and we sat down to lunch. The trout were pan sized and delicious. So were the sourdough biscuits and sourdough pancakes that Frank cooked on his big wood-burning stove. Pancakes come in all thicknesses, but I'd always thought that thick ones were likely to be uncooked in the middle. Frank's pancakes were the thickest I'd ever eaten. They sat on the griddle like little pillows, yet they were perfect all the way through. There must have been some secret, either in the temperature of his griddle or in the sourdough culture that he had kept going for many years. After trout, biscuits, and pancakes, there came strawberries from Frank's garden. It was another feast.

As we ate, I asked Frank a few questions to get him to tell about his background. He had spent most of his life as a prospector and a miner. His stooped back was the result of bending over as he swirled his pan, looking for the glint of gold at its bottom. He had been in the Yukon gold rush and had climbed the infamous Chilkoot Pass. He had also been at the strike at Thunder Mountain.

"Where was that?" I asked.

"Not far from here," he said. "Less than fifty miles due west. There was a big gold strike. The damn fools built the mining town right against the mountain. The mountain was always making noises; that's why they called it Thunder Mountain. One night, the mountainside let go, wiped out half the town. The other half was drowned out because the landslide dammed the creek."

"And you were there?" I asked.

"Oh yes, I was there; saw the whole thing."

"That must have been rough."

"Damn rough."

"Wasn't there a book called *Thunder Mountain*?" I asked.

"Sure was," he said. "Zane Grey wrote the book, but I gave him the whole story."

"Zane Grey. You knew Zane Grey?" I asked.

"Sure did, used to guide for him."

"What was he like?" I asked.

"Shit! Pure shit!"

Frank's answer startled me. "What was the problem?"

"For one thing, he went back on a promise. He had a nice fly rod and I admired it. He said it was mine and he'd give it to me as soon as he headed back to California. Well, he never did give it to me. The other thing was that story about Thunder Mountain. When he found out I'd been there, seen the whole thing, he had me sit down with his two secretaries and tell them the story. He had those two women, they did everything for him, even heated stones to keep his feet warm. I wasn't sure I wanted to tell a couple of women everything about Thunder Mountain, but they said to go ahead, nothing would bother them, so I just told them the whole story and they took it all down. I don't know if they wrote the book or he did, but he made a lot of money out of it, and out of the movie, too, and I never got a red cent."

I didn't know if Zane Grey deserved this venom, but Frank's grudge was monumental. His last comment, before I got him off the subject of Zane Grey, was, "Seems to me he wasn't any different from any other Indian."

I told Frank of my experiences on the upper river and of my stay at Ed Budell's cabin on Pungo Creek. I asked about the boy who had been killed in the plane crash. Frank had witnessed the tragedy.

"They took off from the strip down here. There was engine trouble, and the plane crashed on the far side of the river. You could stop and have a look at it after you leave here."

"I'll do that," I said, and then asked, "And the pilot wasn't hurt?"

"Scratches, that's all," said Frank. "Of course, the pilot was in the back seat and the kid was in front. That could have made the difference. I felt a little funny about it, because it might have been me that was going out, or Milt Hood, or anyone else living along the river."

I could see the drift of his thoughts and said, "It's strange that of all the people in the canyon, the least useful one should have been in the plane at the time."

"That's true," said Frank, "but all the same, life was as dear to him as it is to you and me."

That put me in mind of the dangers I'd be facing in the next few days. I asked Frank if he'd ever been in the Impassable Canyon.

"Oh yes," he said. "I've been through the canyon in winter, on snowshoes, on the shore ice."

"That sounds like a dangerous proposition," I commented.

"Perhaps, but it's a short way to get from here to the outside."

"Did you by any chance meet up with the hermit, Earl Parrott?"

"No, but I can't say I'd want to. Sometimes people who are alone that much can get pretty strange."

I asked if Parrott were still living in the canyon.

"I don't know," Frank said, "but my advice is not to go looking for him. Remember that the most dangerous animal you can meet is the one with two legs."

"Can you remember anything about the rapids, any particularly bad spots I should look out for?" I had carried the last few sheets of my map up to the cabin and now spread them out on the table. Frank studied them for a while, then pointed to a place where the river narrowed and took a turn to the right. It was marked Redside Rapid.

"Right there, the river goes down pretty steep among big

boulders. That's one to look out for, but there are a lot of bad places. My advice is that if you're not sure of a rapid, take the time to carry around it. The Impassable Canyon is no place to take a spill. But I guess you can figure that out. If you've made it this far you can get through."

I thanked Frank for his advice and his hospitality and got up to leave, but before going, I asked him to direct me to his outhouse. He showed me where it was and also showed me a new one he was building, a magnificent structure, made of heavy logs, with a pit under it at least twelve feet deep.

"Why so deep?" I asked.

Frank showed me a row of glass jars on a shelf at the front of his cabin. As he dug the pit under his new outhouse, he had taken samples of earth every few feet. The samples were waiting for him to test with his gold-miner's pan. What had started as a simple pit under an outhouse was turning into a mine shaft. Once started, Frank was reluctant to give up digging. The next shovelful might be pay dirt.

"Did you ever make a really rich strike?" I asked.

Frank shook his head. "No," he said. "And I went all sorts of places, anyplace I thought there might be gold. I took chances. Sometimes I wonder why I spent those nights sleeping in the rain and the snow. Most folks would call it crazy foolishness, but I'm glad I did it. I guess I just did it for the hell of it."

When I was about to leave, Frank urged me to stay the night. "The rest will do you good," he said. "You've got to be in top shape when you come to the Impassable Canyon."

"That's kind of you," I said, "but I'm sure I've recovered from those chills I had on the upper river. Besides, I'm already behind schedule. I've got just five days to catch my train in Shoshone."

I thanked him again and started down to the river. His last words to me were, "Just keep your nerve, and you'll make it."

Buoyed up by Frank's encouraging words, I hiked downhill to my boat and then started downriver, keeping an eye on the left bank for the wrecked plane. I soon spotted the orange and red wings and fuselage a short way back from the river in a flat area that was dotted with boulders and a few pines. I pulled into shore, climbed the bank, and walked over to the wreck. It appeared that the plane, which was a biplane with two open cockpits, had spun in at a steep angle, burying its nose in the ground. Then it had flopped back on its tail. There was a good deal of dried blood on the instrument panel of the front cockpit. As I turned to go, a sparrow hawk dove at me, scolding. It circled above my head until I was back in my boat and on my way downriver. I suppose it had a nest nearby and that explained its behavior, but somehow the hawk seemed connected to the story of the young man who had spent his days in Ed Budell's cabin, reading pulp westerns. At least, the bird must have been present, screaming in terror, when the plane fell out of the sky.

From Loon Creek onward the canyon walls became steeper and rockier. Whitewater boaters learn to expect changes in a river whenever they see a change in the topography of the surrounding valley, so I was on the lookout for difficult rapids. However, I found no serious obstacles until nine miles beyond Loon Creek where I came to a waterfall named Tappan Falls after a ranch family that had settled in the area.

I landed and scouted the falls very carefully. The drop was about five feet, more perpendicular in some places than in others. The greater volume of water went down on the right. I doubted that I could get through the reversal at the bottom. The drop on the left was more abrupt, but I thought I could handle it better. The line of the falls across the river was uneven. Left of center the falls angled downstream, and at the inflection point a large rock jutted downstream from the falls. My plan was to approach the falls close to the left bank and then cut to the right and go over the drop just to the left of the big rock. It looked like a reasonable route, particularly since I could guide on the big rock. I didn't want to go over the falls at some unplanned location. I was able to follow my route except that when I dropped down beside the rock, my bow skidded into the eddy below the rock and I did a super-fast and completely unscheduled eddy turn. Fortunately, I remained upright. I backed out of the eddy and away from the turbulence that filled the right half of the river.

Two miles beyond the falls I passed Camas Creek, a major tributary, and three miles below that came to Aparejo Point, a place where the river turned sharply to the left and passed through a narrow opening between steep cliffs. As might be expected, there was a good rapid in the opening. It was like no

other rapid I found on the Middle Fork. It had a drop followed by a wave train, but whereas most standing waves are shaped roughly like pyramids or haystacks, these waves extended from side to side, almost the whole width of the river, like an old-fashioned washboard on a giant scale. The distance from crest to crest was long enough so that my boat rode to the top and sank to the bottom without shipping water. I was appreciating the appeal of the Middle Fork; each rapid is different from the previous one.

"Aparejo" is a Spanish word for a type of pack saddle that was used in the early days, though how it came to be attached to this place I have no idea. Spanish place names are not common in Idaho. My maps showed that this narrowing of the canyon had been picked by the 1930 United States Geological Survey team as a prime site for building a dam. The plan was to build a four-hundred-foot-high concrete structure. Because the canyon was very narrow, the dam would have also been only four hundred feet across at the top. It would have backed up the river at least to Loon Creek. Tappan Falls would have been underwater. As I bobbed through the long waves of the rapid, I looked up at the cliffs and imagined cranes hauling great buckets of concrete, and the whir of machinery replacing the noise of the rapids. I hoped it would never happen.

Three miles beyond Aparejo Point, I stopped to look over the remains of Mormon Ranch. The ruins of the ranch buildings were on the right bank at a place where the river swung to the left to skirt a grassy bench that must have been a good pasture for cattle. I viewed the ruins with the feeling that I was close to a grim relic of western history. Slim had told me that during the Nez Percé War, a band of Indians had started at the headwaters of the Middle Fork and had followed the canyon downstream. Coming upon this ranch, occupied by a family of Mormons, the Indians had massacred all the settlers: men, women, and children. I might have spared myself those sombre thoughts if I'd known the truth. All of the action in the Nez Percé War took place much farther north and at a time when there were no white settlers in the Middle Fork canyon. The Nez Percé War was before the Sheepeater War. The ranch was really abandoned because the rancher had more than one wife, and he was hauled off to jail. That probably occurred in the 1880s when Mormons were much persecuted in Idaho. One of the politicians responsible for this persecution was Fred Dubois, a Yale graduate who moved to Idaho and who served twice in the U. S. Senate. Perhaps he was a distant relative of mine. As I looked at the remains of the cabins, I should have been contemplating the intolerance of my own kin and not the savagery of the Indians.

Just ahead was the Crandall Ranch. Zee had stopped there on his trip and had been full of praise for Mrs. Crandall's hospitality. The ranch buildings were on a bench and were hidden from the river. A bridge, built after my map was drawn, somewhat confused me, but by studying the twists of the river and the shape of the canyon, I was able to stop before going too far. The light was beginning to fail as I shouldered my duffle bag and climbed the bank.

I found Mrs. Crandall in her chicken house. I explained that I was on my way down the river, and asked if I might spend the night. I also told her that I was a friend of Zee Grant's and asked if she remembered him from two years before.

"Of course I remember him," she said, "and as for you spending the night, if I only had one bunk, I'd let you use it, and I'd sleep in here with the chickens."

Mrs. Crandall was about Frank Allison's age and just as lively. She had a reputation for fearlessness. Once a stranger came to her ranch house with the intention of robbing her. She got the drop on him with her rifle and chased him down to the banks of the Middle Fork, where she forced him to wade and swim across the river. It must have been quite low at the time.

I sat with Mrs. Crandall at supper, which consisted of vegetables and salad. Later we were joined by a young Forest Service ranger, Bob Lyon, and his wife Doris. They had recently been married. Doris was from New Orleans, a beautiful girl, but not the stereotype of the delicate southern belle. The canyons and mountains of Idaho must have been quite a change for her, but I was sure that she would adapt easily.

Sitting in the kitchen, which was illuminated by a kerosene lamp, we talked about the river and the people who had gone down it. Mrs. Crandall showed me a postcard she had received from Zee. He had made a great impression on her, as he did on everyone. As for Hindman, he had stopped at the ranch the afternoon before. He was still more than a day ahead of me.

I asked about Parrott. Was he still in the canyon? Bob Lyon had heard that after the 1939 expedition, Dr. Frazier had located the old man's brother who somehow was able to reach the hermit and persuade him to spend his last years on the outside. Bob had another bit of information about Parrott. The hermit was so wary of human contact that when he needed supplies, he would use a form of barter that required no face-to-face encounter. He would leave gold at a special place beside the Main Salmon River. The next sweep-scow captain running the river would stop, take the gold, and leave supplies.

To conserve kerosene, the party broke up early. I went outside to the bunkhouse and turned in for the night. I was the only one there; there was no need for Mrs. Crandall to sleep with the chickens.

Next morning after breakfast, Mrs. Crandall handed me a lettuce sandwich and a hard-boiled egg for my lunch. She said she had no meat to put in the sandwich and none for herself. She added, rather dolefully, that a doctor had told her that she must eat more meat or she would run the risk of being seriously ill. Not wanting this to happen, I gave her the rest of my ham; she would be able to get a few good meals from it. Besides the sandwich and the egg, I now had only a few bouillon cubes, a small amount of pancake flour, enough butter to grease the frying pan, and some coffee. That would have to do until I got out of the canyon. I thanked Mrs. Crandall for her hospitality and went on my way.

One of my original plans for the trip had been to make a record of it on movie film, and for that purpose I had brought along a rather ancient sixteen-millimeter camera. The plan would have worked nicely for a three-man trip, but not for a solo run. Now I saw the possibility of getting some footage as a record of the trip. A mile and a half below Crandall Ranch there was a rapid, not one of the most arduous on the Middle Fork but still a respectable rapid, quite long and with an interesting combination of rocks and waves. It is now called Haystack Rapid, and in the years since I ran it, it has claimed at least one life. I asked Bob Lyon if he would film me going through this rapid, and he agreed.

Besides Bob and Doris, another person was present to watch me go through the rapid. This was a young man who had been an assistant boatman, meaning the man at the rear sweep, on big freight scows running the Main Salmon. He had never seen a foldboat and was curious to see how it behaved in the whitewater.

We walked down the trail along the left bank and found a spot that commanded a good view of the rapid. Just across from us, two enormous boulders shouldered the water aside. One had marks like the wrinkles on the nose of an elephant; the other looked like the head of a giant lizard. These boulders provided a good background for the nearer rocks and waves, and in fact they have been much photographed over the years. I worked out my course, told Bob when to start and when to stop filming, and then walked back to my boat.

The rapid was the longest continuous stretch of whitewater I had run since Powerhouse on the upper river. The current was very swift, with a number of rocks just breaking the surface. I ran close to some of the rocks and down a slot between a pair of them so as to add interest to the film. It was a good, fast run. At the end, I had trouble finding a landing spot and had to settle for a long walk back to my patient camera crew.

"What did you think of it?" I asked the assistant boatman.

"I was surprised at how that little boat took the waves," he said, "but I don't think you ran it very conservatively."

"I'll be conservative from now on," I promised.

"You'd better, from what I've heard of the Impassable Canyon," he said, then asked, "Have you ever broken up one of those boats?"

"No," I answered, "but I've seen it happen often enough. You get anything broadside to a rock, and the river will wrap you right around it."

"Don't I know," he said. "I was on a scow that hit a boulder, swung broadside, and broke up."

"One of those forty-foot Salmon River scows?"

"That's right. Took about fifteen seconds and it was kindling."

"That must have been quite a sight," I said.

I thanked them for taking the film. We shook hands and they wished me luck on the last lap of my journey. Carrying the camera, I headed back to the boat.

I still have the film showing me running Haystack. It is of poor quality, scratched and overexposed, but recently I put it to good use. I projected it, photographed the projection, and had the photos enlarged. I sent picture sequences to the Forest Service office in Challis and to John Bryant of Salmon, Idaho. River Manager Ted Anderson, of the Forest Service, and Bryant are both extremely familiar with the Middle Fork and recognized every rock in my pictures of Haystack. They both estimated that I was on the river at not much below five thousand cubic feet per second. The Forest Service has designated four ranges of water flow. Below seven hundred CFS, the river is considered too low to be navigated in its upper reaches except by small boats. From seven hundred to forty-five hundred is a range called "normal hazard." From forty-five to sixty-eight, the range is called "extremely hazardous, for professional boatmen and experienced amateurs only." Above sixty-eight hundred, the designation is "suicidal." Zee, from the photos and description in his article, must have been on the river in the low stage. I was running somewhere near the boundary between normal hazard and extremely hazardous, though when I started down Marsh Creek six days earlier, I must have been clearly within the extremely hazardous range. A week before that, when Ed, Stu, and I made our first attempt, the Middle Fork was undoubtedly in the suicidal range. We were fortunate to have quit when we did.

9

Impassable Canyon

No more than twenty-seven miles of distance and six hundred feet of drop now lay between me and Gus Peebles's cabin at the junction of the Middle Fork and the Main Salmon. The average drop was twenty-two feet per mile, nothing compared to the steepness of the upper river, but I knew that there were other factors that would make this last section more difficult than any I had faced. The Middle Fork was by now a much larger river, carrying an impressive volume of water. The middle section, which I had just completed, was typically two hundred feet wide, sometimes wider, though narrower at a few spots like Tappan Falls and Aparejo Point. My map showed me that in the canyons ahead the river was, at its widest, perhaps one hundred and fifty feet, and at some spots much narrower, seventy-five or even fifty feet. The river, pressed between closer banks, must compensate by running deeper and swifter. That would mean bigger waves and more powerful eddies.

The map gave another clue to the changed character that would make these twenty-seven miles more formidable than the upper river. Starting with Haystack, the map had little hatch marks to indicate the location of rapids. There were three or four such rapids per mile. The implication, and this agreed with what Zee had told me, was that each quarter or third of a mile, the river would drop five to seven feet rather abruptly, with calmer stretches between drops. It was reasonable to think that in some rapids the drop would be much more. I assumed that these more imposing rapids were the ones that the cartographers had given names. One such rapid, Hancock, had a notation beside it on the map: "12 foot fall." A much-narrowed river, abruptly dropping twelve feet, was something to look forward to with a tense feeling in the stomach.

There was other information on the map: From this point on, there were fifteen spots marked "camping place." This indicated that only once every two miles was it possible to find space beside the river flat enough to make camp, which in turn was why Zee and his companions had run a portion of the Impassable Canyon after nightfall. Their maps had been lost in Zee's upset at Sulfur Slide, and they thought the passage through the Impassable Canyon was much shorter than it actually is. They got a late start from Crandall Ranch. When light in the canyon started to fail, they could find no place to camp and so kept going, hoping that the end of the canyon was just ahead. They ran some of the worst rapids, including Redside, by picking out the main channel by flashlight, pointing the bow downstream, and trusting the current to get them through. Before they slept that night, they had a strange encounter with Earl Parrott, and Coleman Nimick once more wrapped his boat around a rock. I wanted no such adventures and was glad I had the maps to help me find a camping spot.

Also on the map was an item of historical interest. Barnard Creek is a small creek that comes in beside Haystack Rapid.

The next creek downstream, also a small one, is Short Creek. At this point, the map has a notation: "From Short Creek to Mouth, the stream was traversed with rubber boats. Most of the rapids are indicated either by name or by the conventional sign." Somewhere there must be a diary or a set of field notes that would tell the story of that 1930 trip through the Impassable Canyon. In answer to my recent inquiries, a librarian of the U. S. Geological Survey has searched its archives for relevant information, but without success. The map remains the only link to this piece of whitewater history, and the map has been out of print for many years. I have a copy, the one I carried with me on the Middle Fork, and which on the morning of June 28, 1942, I folded carefully and tucked inside my shirt so that I could have quick access to it as I went down the river.

As I paddled downstream, I could look ahead and see that the canyon walls were growing steeper, with much exposed rock. This told me, even without my maps, that there would be a change in the river. Indeed there was. Each of the short, steep rapids had to be studied carefully in advance, more often than not from the bank. Because of the greater volume of water and the sharper drops, all the river's features were exaggerated in size. Leading into drops there were often large souse holes. A souse hole is formed by a submerged rock. In a way it's a narrow waterfall in the middle of a river. Water rushing over the top of the rock plunges over the downstream side, then curls back up in the same hydraulic jump or reversal that occurs on the downstream side of a falls or a dam. The difference is that in the case of a souse hole, water rushing by the sides of the rock closes in the sides of the souse hole, making it a foam-filled pit in the middle of the river. You can bridge over, or plow through a small souse hole with impunity. Modern kayakers sometimes play games with souse holes, standing their boats on end in the turbulence, but even that has a limit. A souse hole formed by a great volume of water passing with high velocity over a large boulder is a dangerous obstacle.

I had encountered large waves in the upper river, but they

were now much more common. There were diagonal waves, thrown out by rock abutments on the side of the river or by rocks that shouldered their way above water level. There were also large standing waves where the fast water at the outrun of a drop surged into the slower water below. These waves often extended in long trains of successively smaller waves. Below each rock or projection of the cliff thrust into the river from the bank there were powerful eddies, water swirling clockwise against the right bank and counterclockwise against the left bank. These features of the river succeeded one another and combined in endless variation. They were all forms I had been dealing with on the upper river, and even in my experience on New England rivers. Anyone can study such forms by watching water run down a gutter. Only here the scale was bigger, and scale can be important. Being familiar with domestic cats doesn't prepare one to face a tiger.

At each drop the most important decision was the point of entry, where to commit to the fast water, probably not with the main current because of the size of the waves, nor with some easy path at the top of a rapid that would lead into trouble farther down. Once the entry point was decided, there was sometimes a problem of getting there. If the drop had to be entered from the left but I had scouted from the right, then I would make a quick dash across the river; between rapids I couldn't paddle upstream for a leisurely crossing because the current was too strong. Once properly lined up for the drop, and as the boat accelerated over the edge, I would have a brief moment to look ahead and correlate the more-or-less stationary and understandable pattern that I had seen from the bank with the confusion ahead of me. Now only the tops of waves would be visible against a background of more waves. Souse holes would be indicated by a horizontal line, a boundary between darker water pouring over a lip and white turbulence below. Once in the rapid, my problem would be to stick to my predetermined course and to deal with rocks, souse holes, waves, and eddies as they came upon me. Sometimes I would paddle ahead, sometimes I would backpaddle, but more often than not I would just stabilize the boat with my paddle. At the bottom of the rapid, I would swing into an eddy, pull up to the bank, bail out the boat, and evaluate my run.

The worst water I encountered that morning was at Senk Rapid. It was longer than most of the others and very mean in the center. Fortunately, I was able to pick out a safe course on the left. Senk Rapid has long since been renamed Jack Creek Rapid after the nearby Jack or Jackass Creek. Senk was certainly a peculiar name for a stretch of whitewater, but I have a theory as to its origin. In the lower left corner of each of my USGS maps, there is the notation: "Topography by L. L. Bryan and W. C. G. Senkpiel." Perhaps "Senk" is what the survey crew called Senkpiel, and perhaps he had some mishap at this spot. I can imagine him crawling out of the river, very wet, and someone calling, "Hey Senk, let's name this one after you." It's a pity the name hasn't stuck.

In spite of stops to check out rapids, I made good progress, and in a few hours I looked ahead and saw the suspension bridge that carried the trail from the right side of the river over to the left and up Big Creek. Trail and bridge had been built by the Civilian Conservation Corps at some time in the thirties. Before that, the trail to Big Creek had left the river at Barnard Creek and gone across country. I had been glad of the trail on the right bank for the nine miles I had come that morning. It had offered an escape route which from now on would be missing. I was reluctant to push on past this link to the outside world. For the moment, I had an excuse to stop: lunch. I landed on a gravel bar of river-smoothed stones and boulders of all sorts of colors and textures. Many of them had the large-crystal structure of granite. I supposed that these rocks had come from every portion of the canyon and from many of the tributaries that fed the Middle Fork. I selected a flat-sided rock and sat with my back against it, facing upriver, absorbing the strong sunlight, and also protected by the rock from the upstream wind. I felt completely recovered from my chills of the upper river, and I was grateful for the good weather of the past few days and for the hospitality of the people who lived along the river. As I wolfed down the lettuce sandwich, the cheese, and the hardboiled egg Mrs. Crandall had given me, I imagined that at that moment she was eating a slice of the ham I had given her. I hoped she enjoyed it.

After lunch I delayed my departure as long as possible. I studied my maps. I had eighteen miles to go with a drop of three hundred and eighty feet. Could I cover that many miles and descend that many feet in one afternoon, or would I have to find a camping spot in the canyon and dine on soup cubes and pancakes? I wouldn't find out by sitting with my back against a rock. I heaved myself to my feet and went back to my boat. I made sure that my duffle bag was securely tied in. Then I slipped the boat into the water, climbed into the cockpit, swung into the current, and drifted past the mouth of Big Creek which roared in from the left. This was the beginning of the Impassable Canyon.

The river turned to the right, went down one of its smaller steps, and surged along between low but steep cliffs. Above these cliffs, the canyon angled upward with grass-and sage-covered slopes punctuated by ponderosa pines. Above these slopes were more cliffs. I looked up and saw two bald eagles circling above the river. I had seen many of these birds in Maine, two above the Housatonic River in Connecticut, and one over Moriches Bay on the south shore of Long Island. That very bird, I was told by a naturalist cousin of mine, was the bird that graced the old twenty-five-cent piece, a realistic design long since abandoned for a stylized eagle. Seeing these great birds had always taken my breath away, but these two eagles, soaring between the cliffs of the Middle Fork, seemed to epitomize the spirit of the wilderness. They accentuated my feeling that I was in a place as untouched by man as any that could be found. One of the eagles passed directly overhead, not more than fifty feet up. As he glided by, he turned his head to the side, no doubt to get a better look at the strange creature on the surface of the water. He slid past on the wind, and my attention was taken by the next drop.

The river began to twist. The cliffs closed in, high and steep. The grassy slopes narrowed to the dimensions of ledges. Here I saw something completely unexpected—a primitive ladder connecting two ledges on the face of the cliff on the right side of the river. The upstream ledge was the lower one. It slanted up out of the river, though at a lower stage of water it was probably dry. Where this ledge gave out, the ladder reached to a higher ledge. I wondered who had constructed the ladder. It

was my impression that Parrott's secret trail was much farther downstream and connected his placer camp to the Main Salmon. Some other prospector must have pushed his trail down this portion of the canyon. I decided that even with this faint trail, I would not like to work my way along the cliffs and talus slopes of the canyon. I remembered Slim Hendrick's warning, "If you spill in the Impassable Canyon, hang onto your boat. That's the only way you can get out of there."

Without any specific knowledge of the cubic feet per second on which I was riding, I still had a sense that the river was at a high stage. Along any riverbank there is a scoured area that defines high water. Above that there may be occasional logs that have been deposited by the floods of record years. Below such large logs and below the line of scouring, there are often fresh deposits of branches, grass, and other debris left by recent crestings of the river. Still farther down, the banks may become less steep and there may even be exposed-silt or gravel-beach areas. By looking at the banks as well as at the water itself, the river runner can judge the relative stage at which the river is flowing. All the signals suggested to me that the river was high, but that it had been much higher. Not long after seeing the ladder, I came upon a log perched on top of a big rock on the right side of the river. The log was crosswise to the current and perfectly horizontal. It reminded me of a spar on a square-rigged ship. I passed beside the rock and directly under the log, which was at least ten feet above my head. The flood that deposited that log must have been an awesome sight.

Still, there was a great deal of water. On the upper river I had been very aware of the high volume in the river and of the additions from each side creek. On the middle river, all new water seemed to come from major tributaries such as Marble, Loon, and Camas creeks. The small creeks were much dryer, and I had a sense that the water level of the river was dropping. Here in the Impassable Canyon, I again had the sense that the river was very high and that water was pouring into it, not only from Big Creek, which brought in a tremendous volume, but also from innumerable small creeks on both sides of the river. This wasn't surprising because there were mountains just back from the river. The peaks were masked by the canyon walls, but up there were snowfields, exposed to the late-June sun. There were also timberline lakes, ice now melting and draining into creeks that flowed toward the Middle Fork. Meltwater streamed into the canyon; every small creek was a torrent. At one place, water came out of a hole or cleft in the rock wall and fell directly into the river. At another, a thin stream of water fell from the top of the canyon wall onto the talus slope, a drop of hundreds of feet. Behind the falls was a great cave, an amphitheatre cut out of the cliff wall. I would have liked to climb the talus slope to that cave, perhaps even camp there, but there wasn't time. I had to be content to look up briefly at the falls and cave and then drift on.

The canyon was a vast and exciting place. I had seen many pictures of the Grand Canyon and of other canyons that were cut through sedimentary rock. This canyon was very different. Because it was cut through granite, it had none of the regularized talus slopes and cliffs that are formed by a river cutting down through alternating layers of hard and soft rock. Here the shapes of the canyon walls were less predictable. On one side of the river or the other there was often a talus slope, a great jumble of rocks slanting up from the river to the base of a cliff that would then soar upward for a thousand feet or more. Sometimes a vertical cliff or a steep slanting face of rock would plunge directly into the river. At other places there might be a narrow bench above the river, and behind that a cliff. The total depth of the canyon was between three and four thousand feet, though it was seldom possible to see all the way to the top from the river.

I was surprised by the amount of vegetation in the canyon. There was a great deal of bare rock but there were also many trees. Deciduous trees, not the same birches and maples I knew from New England, but similar trees, clustered at the mouth of every creek. Stately ponderosa pines grew wherever their roots could find sufficient soil, sometimes close to the water's edge and sometimes on ledges high on the canyon wall. The air in the canyon was sweet with the scent of pine, sage, fresh grass, and spring wildflowers, vegetation that grew on the benches above the river and in patches of soil between boulders on the talus slope.

There were bighorn sheep and mountain goats in the canyon; Frank Allison had told me that. Zee had seen wild horses near the confluence with the Main Salmon. There must have been a few mountain lions. I was hopeful that if I looked carefully at the ledges on the canyon walls, I would see some of these larger animals, but I saw none, perhaps because my eyes had to be on the river. When I looked up at the slopes, it was only briefly.

Whenever I got out of my boat to scout a rapid, I was aware that the talus slope, with its rocks and its interspersed vegetation, was a home for many small birds, rodents, and reptiles. In my concentration on the river, I paid them little attention. Once, while scouting a rapid, I had an encounter with a snake. I was climbing high on the talus, trying to find a good spot to look down on the whitewater, when I realized that just in front of me, and on a rock I intended to use for my next step, was a good-sized snake. I couldn't see his tail, and I don't remember the shape of his head, so I have no idea whether it was a rattlesnake or a harmless gopher snake. Whichever it was, the snake was absolutely motionless, waiting for supper to wander by. That was his privilege. I backtracked and climbed higher on the slope, bypassing the snake.

My progress for the first four miles beyond Big Creek was steady and also reassuring in that I was able to pick sneak routes around most of the bad places. Even Porcupine, a long rapid like Senk, was passed safely. The next really bad place after Porcupine was Redside. Here the river narrowed, turned to the right, and dropped abruptly, smashing over and between enormous boulders. I landed well above the drop, on the right side of the river, and I scrambled along the bank until I could see the drop from below. No wonder Frank Allison had been impressed with this place, even in winter. I looked the rapid over very carefully and found a path on the far right where I could drop down in two steps. The route would keep me out of the main current and the more vicious water in the center. The only problem was that the first fall was so abrupt that if the curve of the bow hitting the water below was slanted in the wrong direction, the boat could slew around as it had at Tappan Falls; but here I wouldn't just be making an eddy turn, I'd be going over the second drop sideways. I would have to go over the first drop with the tilt of the bow calculated to take me into the second drop.

The route I had chosen was probably available only at high water, a sneak route of the type that had served me so well. The problem with continually picking such paths was that I didn't get enough practice in the strong hydraulics of the main current. I was running the river more by intellect than by reflex. Sooner or later I'd have to face one of these drops without the benefit of the bypass route.

I went back to my boat, climbed in, and drifted into the slot between boulders that marked my route. I went over the drop, the bow falling sharply and landing at just the right angle to carry me into the second drop. It was an exciting passage, and I was pleased to have executed it according to plan and without shipping any water. If I could run Redside so easily, what was there to worry about? In an inflated frame of mind, I headed for the next rapid.

The drop was coming up fast. If I wanted to land above it, I'd have to make an instant decision. It looked like a single short drop. Why not just run it and avoid the tedious process of scouting from the bank? The moment in which I could have reached an eddy along the bank passed and I was committed. Close ahead, the current was divided by a large rock that just broke the surface. Most of the water went down on the left, and I could see large standing waves downstream on that side. On the right the passage was narrow and might lead into a jumble of rocks that could trap me in my boat. I decided to slide down with the main current, hoping for a clear run between the eddy below the rock and the haystacks. I guessed the shape of the rock, judging that if it were round, there would be a smooth ramp of water going down close to the rock. I lined up my boat with this imagined ramp. Unfortunately, the rock wasn't round; it was more a rough block, with water spilling over its shoulder. When I saw my mistake, it was too late to get into the main current on the left. The bow pointed down at an impossible angle toward a foaming pit below the rock. I had the thought that what I needed was a submarine, not a foldboat.

The bow plunged into the boil of foam, and instantly the boat was wrenched over with me underneath, head down. A good modern kayaker might have rolled up, but I had neither the training nor the equipment for that maneuver. My only option was to bail out, and that proved very difficult. As I struggled to get free of the small cockpit, I wondered if I would drown, and if so, how far downstream would the debris drift before being caught in an eddy, and how long would it be before anyone found out what had happened.

With a mighty struggle, I broke loose and came to the surface, just in time to get a breath of air before being pulled under again and dragged through a long series of standing waves. In a hundred yards, I was in calmer water but could see another rapid ahead. "Now you've done it," I said to myself, but then remembered Slim's words, "... hang onto your boat... " I looked around and discovered the boat a few yards upstream, floating bottom up. Although I was exhausted and was having a hard time breathing, I slid up on one end of the boat. Then I spotted the paddle, got off the boat, retrieved the paddle, slid up on the boat again, straddled it, and paddled for the right bank. The boat moved sluggishly, but it did respond, and I knew that I could reach shore before the next rapid. As I was closing in on the shore, looking for an eddy, I received a sharp blow on my left shinbone. The strong current had taken me directly over a submerged rock. A few more strokes brought me into an eddy just above the next rapid. There was a small rocky beach, and as I came up to it, a coyote trotted away among the rocks of the talus slope. I supposed he had been watching the whole show.

I beached the boat and drained out most of the water by alternately lifting the bow and the stern, doing it gently so as not to break the wooden framework with the weight of the water.

Then I rolled the boat rightside up to evaluate the damage. The spray deck was broken in a dozen places. For a hundred miles it had kept out most of the water that had poured over the bow of the boat as I plowed through waves. It wasn't a perfect design, but it had done the job. Now it was too broken to be repaired. I would have to abandon it and run the remaining thirteen miles of the canyon, including Hancock with its twelve-foot drop, with a nearly seven-foot-long open cockpit. It would be almost as vulnerable as running in an open canoe.

I pulled the remains of the spray deck off the boat and checked for other damage or loss. The boat was intact. The duffle bag was still in place and completely dry on the inside. The few items of loose gear, including my bailing can, were still in the boat. I checked inside my shirt. My map was still there, although soaked. Waterproof matchbox and emergency chocolate were still in my pockets, but my knife was gone from its sheath. I had been fond of that knife. It was Swedish, with a handle carved from curly birch, and I had bought it at the 1939 New York World's Fair. Well, I could do without it as I no longer had a ham to slice. Except for the spray deck and the knife, my equipment had survived the upset very well.

Physically, I was also in reasonable shape. I was grateful that it was a warm day. After stripping, wringing out my clothes, and putting them on again, I felt no ill effects from my dunking in the cold water. My leg hurt badly. The blow had torn my jeans and abraded the skin. There was some blood and the leg was beginning to swell, but I could put weight on it and move about, so I assumed it wasn't broken.

My state of mind had not survived as well. I knew that I had had a very close call and that it was entirely due to my own overconfidence; that confidence was now pretty well shaken. I knew also that very soon I'd have to get back into my boat and head downriver, but I was very loath to get started. To steady my nerves, I dug my .22-caliber automatic out of my duffle bag, and I banged away at a small stick that I had set up on a driftwood log. This diversion, the need to hold the sights steady, perhaps even the reports echoing in the canyon, had the desired effect. When I sent the stick flying, I felt better prepared to face the river.

In preparation for setting out again, I clambered along the bank to see what was downstream. This was a difficult process because of the pain in my left leg and because just downstream from my landing place the bank narrowed down to a bare minimum under a cliff. I scouted far enough to look over three rapids that came in quick succession. Then I went back to my boat, found that there was still some water in the bottom, and bailed it out. The cockpit looked very vulnerable, and I wondered if I could devise at least a partial spray deck. I experimented with my air mattress. There was no good way to tie it over the opening, but I did wedge it into the front portion of the cockpit to act as a wave deflector. I doubted that it would keep out much water, but it was the best I could do.

Something remained to be done. Suppose I didn't survive the last thirteen miles. I wanted to leave at least some record of my having made it this far, and of having lost my spray deck in an upset. I found a pencil and a piece of paper in my duffle bag, sketched a little map showing where I had upset, and scribbled a brief account of what had happened to me. I then decided that having upset in the drop, I had the right to name it. I would call it Lenore Rapid after the girl whose mother recommended a diet of pancakes for the trip. I added my claim to name the rapid to the note and looked about for a way of preserving the piece of paper. In the duffle bag I found a metal Band-aid box. I dumped the bandages into the duffle bag and stuffed the paper into the box. Next I climbed high enough on a nearby talus slope to avoid any possible flood. On a secure boulder I built a cairn, with the Band-aid box inside. I then placed the remains of the spray deck up against the cairn so that it would be visible from the river. I hoped that the next boatman down the river, perhaps a month or a year or more later, would see the broken spray deck and land to investigate.

It took eighteen years for my message to be found. In the fall of 1960, I received a letter from Stu Gardiner.

Dear Eliot:

FOUND: One antique map near the end of a whitewater trail.

It is a small world, Eliot. Last night, while attending a gathering of friends interested in river treks, the conversation naturally got around to the Middle Fork of the Salmon River, which is our favorite whitewater stream. Our gracious hostess was telling of her experience in getting pitched out of a rubber tub [rubber raft] at Redside Rapids and after swimming out, of finding the above mentioned map in a band-aid container. She produced the container and contents and I was quite surprised to find your signature on the note.

Like I said, it's a small world. It has been quite some time since we drug ourselves out from the Marsh Creek country, although it surely doesn't seem long. That was quite an experience.

The rest of the letter dealt with other whitewater matters not connected with the Middle Fork, but in the margin, Stu had written, "P. S. Whatever happened to the girl you named the rapids after?"

I don't know what became of her, though I wish her well. As might be expected, the rapid is not Lenore Rapid, it's Weber Rapid, named for a river guide who upset there, but long after my passage through the canyon. The same conditions that led to my upset—overconfidence after running Redside and the closeness of the two drops—have led other boaters into the same trap. In 1970 Weber claimed two lives; it came close to taking mine in 1942.

10

The Beast at the Bottom of the Canyon

When I climbed into my boat and pushed off once again, I was full of anxiety about shipping water and swamping. After the first three drops, I had regained some confidence; I had kept the cockpit dry. This was partly because my route kept me out of the larger waves and partly because I used a technique I had learned while canoeing on New England rivers. With an open canoe, you can sometimes keep water from sloshing over the gunwales by deliberately tipping the boat so as to present the bottom of the hull to a wave. This is done by bending sideways at the hips and usually stabilizing with the paddle at the same time. The foldboat had a more rounded bottom than a canoe and so could be rotated relatively easily about its long axis. I had been using the hip-swiveling technique as much as I could for the first hundred miles of my Middle Fork trip, but the small cockpit in my spray deck was too high on my body to allow much side motion. With the spray deck gone, I could lean much farther to either side and could shift my weight more effectively. Losing the spray deck made me more vulnerable to big waves, particularly to a reversal headed straight on, but there was some trade-off in increased control.

On my map, three miles below the site of my upset, there was a notation: "Parrott Placer Camp." It was in this area that Zee and his party had a strange meeting with the hermit. Coming down the canyon in the dark, they saw a large campfire on the right. They landed, and after a search, Rodney Aller found the old man crouched behind a rock, a look of terror on his face. Aller placed his hand on Parrott's shoulder, at which Parrott said, "You'd better get out of here; I've got five pet rattlesnakes." Whether or not they believed him, and in spite of the dark, the foldboaters decided it was prudent to leave. They continued downriver until Nimick wrapped his boat around a rock. Fortunately, they were able to get to shore and find a piece of ground flat enough for camping. In the morning, they patched up Nimick's boat and continued their run through the canyon.

I had heard that Parrott had a vegetable garden and I assumed that it was somewhere up above his placer camp on the right bank. I was pretty sure he was out of the canyon, retired to the outside world, and so I thought I'd try to locate his garden. It would be an interesting find, and some vegetables might still be growing there. When my map told me I was in the vicinity of the placer camp, I landed and started to climb the talus slope, but it was such an extensive jumble of rocks that I doubted I could find anything in it. My leg pained me a good deal, and I was about to give up and head back to the boat when I flushed two spruce grouse. One of them flew across the river, but the other landed on the bottom branch of a pine tree that grew up between the boulders. Here was an opportunity for supper. I went back to the boat for my pistol. When I had climbed back to the tree, the bird was still there, peering at me with concern but without the wits to join its mate on the far side of the river. It was a dark target against a dark background, but I brought the bird down with one shot. I felt guilty because of its reproachful eye, but I was hungry.

Afternoon was fading into evening. I was at the head of a two-mile-long, nearly straight section of canyon. On either side, the cliffs rose two or three thousand feet. Between these walls, the river flowed dark, broken with white every third of a mile where it dropped through a rapid. Somewhere along this corridor I would have to find a place to camp. Back in the boat, I worked my way downstream. When my attention wasn't on the river, I scanned the banks for a place flat enough to lay out a sleeping bag and build a fire. I found nothing until I was nearly at the end of the corridor. Looking to the left, I saw a rocky beach, three tall ponderosa pines, and against the cliff, a small cabin. A cabin at this spot took me by surprise. Zee had told me of finding Parrott on the right bank of the river, so who had built this structure? Whoever had lived here, it was a convenient place to land, there was enough flat ground to camp comfortably, and it was time to get off the river. I landed.

The cabin was unusual, a six-foot cube with a single-pitch roof. The bottom logs were perhaps eighteen inches in diameter but the logs were progressively smaller higher up, suggesting that the builder had used only one or two tree trunks for the job. The logs had been fitted and trimmed by ax and then a door had been saw-cut from the top down to the second course. The cracks between the logs had been stuffed with moss. It was a simple but workmanlike structure. On the inside and against the back wall was a built-in bunk. On the floor were the remains of a small cast-iron stove. On the outside, leaning against the side of the cabin, were several bundles of commercial shingles. From the weathering of the shingles and the rust on the bailing wire, I judged that they had been there at least over the winter. I wondered if they had been dropped off the summer before by a boating party. The cabin itself showed no sign of recent habitation, so I thought it a safe place to camp.

By the time I had gathered wood to build my fire, it was growing dark. My next task was to prepare the grouse. At the age of twelve I had raised chickens, so I knew what to do. I boiled water in my bailing/cooking can and poured the water over the bird. This loosened the feathers so I could pull them out. I had lost my knife but my ax was sharp. I used it to make the necessary cuts to clean the bird, saving the heart, liver, and other edible portions. I cooked a pancake, broke it up and mixed in a soup cube and the giblets. With this mixture I stuffed the grouse, then skewered the bird on a green stick which I supported over the fire on two forked sticks. Full of anticipation, I made soup from my last cube and cooked and ate several pancakes. From time to time I turned the spit. After several pancakes, the bird looked done, but when I tried to bite into it, I found I might as well have bitten into one of the granite rocks that lay about on the ground. Back on the fire it went. To fill the time, I cooked more pancakes and made myself a can of coffee, settling the grounds with cold river water. I had another try at the grouse and was marginally successful. I was able to gnaw a little meat off the legs, but that was all. The breast was like cement. Then I remembered the stuffing. I scooped it out with a stick onto my frying pan and then ate it with my fingers. It was delicious. Whatever juices the bird possessed had seeped into the stuffing, there to make a rich combination with the soup cube and the pancake flour.

As I was licking my fingers in front of my fire, I heard a loud report and then another. I looked around to determine the cause of these noises, which were loud and sharp enough to be explosions and seemed quite close. Except for the coals of my fire, it was dark in the canyon and it was difficult to see anything. Just as I was looking across the fire and in the direction of the river, I heard another report and saw, very dimly, a column of water rise high out of the river and then fall back. Another explosionlike noise sounded and another column of water rose out of the river, evidence that rocks were falling off the cliffs, dropping perhaps a thousand feet directly into the water. I wondered if this was the beginning of a landslide. If so, I was in a very unhealthy location. After one more splash, the bombardment ended, leaving me worried and bewildered.

What had caused the rockfall? There is nothing too unusual about rocks falling off cliffs into a river; many rapids are formed that way. But what was the cause of this specific fall? It couldn't have been wind; the night was clear and cool, with no wind stirring. An earth tremor? I had felt no shifting of the ground as I sat by my campfire. Had the stones been dislodged by bighorn sheep? That was a possibility. Were the rocks dislodged by the action of frost, the freezing of water in cracks, the ice expanding to pry rocks off the cliff face? It seemed unreasonable that five or six rocks would be pried loose in a two-minute time span. I thought of another possibility, a more disturbing one. Was some person up there on the cliff throwing rocks down into the canyon in the direction of the small campfire far below? On that night in 1942, I gave this last theory a low probability, but now, forty years later, I have evidence that makes it a likely explanation.

When I saw the cabin and stopped there for the night, I had no idea who had built it. Because of Zee's warning, "Avoid Hermit, right bank!," and because my map showed Parrott's placer camp several miles upstream from the cabin and on the opposite bank, I assumed that all of Parrott's operations were on the far side of the river. Because I saw the river at high water, it didn't occur to me that at low water a man could safely ferry across on a raft. The truth is that the cabin was one of two built by Earl Parrott. One was close to the river near the mouth of Nugget Creek. The other was two thousand feet higher up the side of the canyon. The 1936 Hatch—Swain—Frazier expedition found the lower cabin. Those men also found a trail, made easier by a series of primitive ladders, leading to the upper cabin. Beside the upper cabin, they found a vegetable garden. What happened next was remembered slightly differently by various members of the expedition, but here is the story as I heard it in 1959 from Bus Hatch.

The men had been living on canned goods since they started down the river, so the fresh vegetables looked very tempting. One expedition member pulled up a carrot and started to eat it, saying, "I guess it's OK. There doesn't seem to be anyone around here."

"Oh yes there is," came a voice from above. Down from a tree came a wild-looking old man, naked but carrying a six-shooter in one hand. There were a few anxious moments before the boatmen were able to make their peace with the old hermit.

Three years later, when Frazier, Swain, Amos Burg, and the others of their party were on the river and approaching Parrott's lower cabin, they thought that bullets were hitting the water. The expedition members were somehow able to make friendly contact with Parrott, but it must have been an uneasy process.

As I went down the river, I asked each person I met if Parrott was still in the Impassable Canyon. The last and what I considered the most authoritative information was that the hermit had moved to the outside. That appears not to have been true. Parrott's brother had attempted to persuade the hermit to leave the canyon, but he stayed on until 1942 when a serious prostate problem forced him to leave and to seek medical care. He moved to Salmon City, lived there for three years, and figured in one more bizarre incident. One night he ran out into the street and discharged his pistol through a window of the home of Captain Harry Guleke, the venerable Salmon River scow pilot. Parrott died on August 15, 1945. He was eighty years old.

There is no way of knowing for sure that Parrott was responsible for the rockfall, but it's easy to visualize the old hermit peering down into the canyon and seeing a campfire near his lower cabin. He shoots his forty-five and rolls rocks off the cliff in an attempt to drive the trespasser away. If that is what happened, I am sorry to have caused him additional pain at a trying time in his life.

During the rockfall, I sat behind the fire, startled, but doing nothing because there was little I could do. I was thankful that the rocks fell in the middle of the river and hoped that none would fall nearer the cabin. On the chance that someone up above was rolling rocks into the canyon, I smothered the fire with sand. This left me in complete darkness except for the faint light from a band of stars defined by the tops of the cliffs on either side of the canyon. I had intended to sleep near the base of the pine tree nearest the cabin but decided that if more rocks were to come plummeting, the cabin would be a safer place to sleep. I felt my way in through the narrow opening, located the bunk, unrolled my sleeping bag, and climbed in. There were no more options for evasive action. I was soon asleep.

Much later I awoke and, looking through a hole in the roof, saw moonlight creeping down the western wall of the canyon. A small cloud of spun silver hung just above the canyon. It was a Surrealist scene. I watched for a while and then went back to sleep.

In the morning the spruce grouse was gone, presumably stolen by a coyote. I hoped he had better luck with the bird than I did. For breakfast, I finished the last of my pancake flour and drank good, strong coffee. From my map, I decided I was at Nugget Creek, just eight and a quarter miles from Gus Peebles's cabin at the junction of the Middle Fork and the Main Salmon. The total drop was one hundred and seventy-five feet, and the map showed it to be distributed in twenty-seven rapids. Five of the rapids had names. They were: Weidner, Ouzel, Rubber, Hancock, and Scoop. I was most concerned about Hancock, with its twelve-foot drop, though Weidner, only a half-mile downstream from Nugget Creek, looked dangerous on the map. The river squeezed down to a fraction of its normal width and turned sharply to the right. I would have to be careful from the very start.

Once in my boat, I dropped through a small rapid, crossed to the right bank, and landed. Weidner was still a quarter of a mile ahead but I didn't risk being drawn into it without having looked it over. Going downstream along the bank on foot wasn't easy. I clambered across slide-rock, waded in hip-deep water under a cliff, and finally climbed a steep bank to reach a spot from which I could see all of the rapid. I was greatly surprised to see that Weidner would be a pushover. I went back upstream, got in my boat, and started down, hugging the right bank. Most of the current was on the left, passing close to a cliff that finally hooked to the right so that the current plowed full force into the rock face. The water at that point seemed to turn under and then deflect to the right. The left side of the river would have been an unhealthy place to be in a boat, but on the right I had a smooth and fast ride. As I came abreast of the cliff with its curling wave, I shot over a gravel bar which was a few feet under water. The bank fell away on the right, revealing a giant eddy—more a whirlpool than an eddy because it was rotating fast enough for the center to be visibly lower than the perimeter. Just to my left was a train of standing waves, but I was on an undisturbed filament of water.

This rapid, which I realized would be much more of a hazard at low water, is now called Upper Cliffside. The new name is very descriptive of the place, but there is a loss in dropping the name of one of the early explorers of the river.

After Weidner, the river turned again to the left and went down a sharp drop that is now called Lower Cliffside. I scouted this rapid thoroughly before I ran it and was equally cautious with all the rapids I came to that morning. I also kept a sharp eye on the current between rapids because I didn't want to be swept unprepared into a major drop. I wanted enough warning to be able to land above it for a closer look. Somewhere ahead was Hancock, and there might be other rapids of equal severity. The map showed me that Hancock came just after a bend to the right. Although the general direction of the river was to the north, there were a number of bends to the right and left. After a few miles, I became a bit uncertain as to which jog of the canyon corresponded to which twist of the river on the map. I became doubly cautious, hugging the inside of the turns and looking ahead for possible landing spots.

I came to a place where the river disappeared around a bend to the right. The velocity of the water increased so much as it approached the bend that I thought it prudent to land and work my way around the corner on foot. I had thought that Hancock was a mile ahead, but this might be the place. I landed on the right, at the foot of a talus slope. From the river, such slopes appeared to be made up of small stones, but at close range the small stones became great boulders. Scrambling over them was always difficult. At this place the best route led diagonally upward, so that when I turned the corner, I was quite high above the river. From that position, I could see that I had been wise to stop where I did; I might have had trouble landing if I had gone any farther, as there were few eddies along the bank. Just downstream from my observation point was a very big rapid.

The rapid was of simple form but awesome because of its proportions, a whitewater classic. As the river swept around the bend, there was a steepening and a narrowing of the channel, so that even before reaching the drop, the water was moving at much more than its usual velocity. Then came a point where the channel was further restricted by large boulders both right and left. The water rushed between these boulders and plunged down a steep incline. Below this drop, the water humped up in a high standing wave, then a trough, another wave, a trough, a wave, and so on for a quarter-mile. On either side of the wave train there was a long eddy, and I could be sure the upstream currents were strong along the banks.

As I looked down on this rapid, I felt that all the others had been insignificant. This was the one that had been waiting for me. It was the great beast at the bottom of the canyon: a dragon. The spines along its back were the successive waves of the wave train.

I was convinced that I was looking down on the mighty Hancock, which I understood to be the most formidable rapid of the river. I was indeed looking at the most formidable drop, but it wasn't Hancock. I was looking at what is now called Rubber Rapid, unmarked on my map, though the name Rubber was applied to a less difficult stretch of water a half-mile upstream. There have been various suggestions as to the reason for naming a rapid Rubber, but I believe it was intended to commemorate the rubber boats used by the 1930 survey team.

After I had spent some time just looking at the rapid and appreciating its dimensions, I began to consider my options. One was to carry around the drop. That looked possible but difficult with my injured leg. It would be a shame, though, to run every inch of the Middle Fork, except Dagger Falls, and not run this rapid. Was there a sneak route? Could I treat this one as I had Redside? I studied the rocks and water along both banks and concluded that no sneak route was possible. I'd have to go down with the main current. Should I go right down through the middle, plowing through the waves? Without a spray deck, I'd surely swamp in that wave train. The only other option was to slip down between the wave train and the eddy, not avoiding the first wave completely, but hitting if off-center and sliding sideways toward the eddy line. I was attempting the same game when I flipped in Weber Rapid, but then I had used guesswork to pick my entry point to the drop. Now, I had at least a good vantage point to scout the rapid, though making the correct approach along my predetermined path would still be a problem. I needed something to help me find the beginning filament of water. As I studied the rapid, I discovered a reference point that would be visible from the river. On the left side and just over the brink of the drop, a black rock protruded from the current. The rock threw into the air a plume of foam much as the cutting edge of a tool in a lathe spins off metal from the piece in the chuck. The black rock would be conspicuous even from water level. I would aim for a point six feet to the right of the rock. That would put me within the main current going over the drop, but near its left boundary. That was the best I could do.

When I got back to the boat, I pushed off right away. There was no point in further mulling over my plan. The black rock was my reference, and I would stick to it. I slid out into the current, rounded the bend in midstream, and then worked to the left. Ahead of me was the drop, coming up fast. I could see the tops of the waves dancing above the line of the drop. To be visible from this angle, the first wave must have been higher than the drop. The river grew steeper; the banks began to close in; there was a noticeable increase in velocity. I spotted the black rock, coming toward me on my left. I took a few strokes to bring my path closer to it, the six feet I had decided upon. Then I was past the rock and shooting over the lip of the drop. As I saw the fall of the water and then its rise in the first wave, I was awed

by its proportions and said, "Good God!" The boat accelerated and dropped under me. There were rocks on my left, a smooth steep chute on my right. I reached bottom, then was thrust into the air by the first wave, bow pointing toward the sky, then sliding to the right, the wrong way. I clawed with my paddle to straighten the boat in the current. Then I was up and over the first wave, down in the trough, up on the second wave, bow slightly to the left with the boat beginning to slide sideways. I rode up on only the shoulder of the third wave, and by the fourth, the boat was on the eddy line. I rode the eddy line far down the wave train, then swung into the eddy for a fast ride upstream close to the bank. I wanted to take a second look at what I'd just come through. When I was near the head of the eddy, I hung onto a rock on the bank and looked at the drop and at the first big wave. Both towered above me. I was sure that this was the ultimate rapid of the river. Having run it gave me a feeling of elation. I was glad to have come through but grateful not to have to do it again. Letting go of the rock, I made a careful turn, rode the eddy line downstream for a second time, and found a quiet place to stop and bail. Even with my open cockpit, I had shipped no more than two quarts of water.

Running the big drop was such a consummate whitewater experience that it would have been simple justice for the rest of the river to be a lazy succession of easy rapids. Unfortunately, the Maker of Rivers doesn't deal in simple justice. Five miles of tough water lay ahead of me, and as I approached the next drop and each successive drop, I resented having to land and scout. I wanted to charge ahead, to run the rest of the river without stopping, to bring the adventure to an end.

I had more sense than to give in to that temptation, though in those last five miles there were rapids I ran with the very minimum of scouting. That was less because of my impatience than because of the shape of the canyon. In this last section of river, the canyon walls closed in, the cliffs often coming down into the water. Perhaps at low water it would have been possible to find a path for scouting ahead along the base of the cliff, but such foot passages were now all drowned out so that I often had to climb quite high for a long view downstream. Once when I had climbed fifty feet up, I found a broad ledge leading downstream, perfect, I thought, for an overlook of a rapid that stretched out at the bottom of a narrow corridor. I followed the ledge and suddenly found myself staring down into a straight-sided cut made by a creek coming in from the left. I had to settle for a long view again.

My memory of those last five miles is not so clear as my memory of other portions of the river. That may be due as much to my state of mind at the time as to the passage of years. I see those rapids in a kaleidoscope of rocks, waves, and steep cliffs. Individual scenes or sensations are clear, but it's not easy to fit them together in sequence. There was one long rapid where a train of standing waves snaked from one side of the river to the other, brushing against both banks. I was forced to cross that wave train. I went through diagonally, letting the boat rock under me, keeping the bottom of the boat against the waves so as to keep water from pouring into the large, open cockpit. On one wave I let the hull tip too far and came close to rolling over. At the bottom of the rapid, I was faced with the choice of going through even larger standing waves or punching through a reversal. The boat was already heavy with water, but I chose the reversal and bulled through, taking on even more water. I was past the rapid, but the boat was dangerously unstable. Very gingerly, I eased into an eddy and up to the bank. I had shipped more water than in any other rapid on the river. I am now sure that this long rapid with the snakelike standing waves was Hancock Rapid, not as spectacular as Rubber Rapid, but one that gave me more trouble.

At another place, the current forced me into a cliff. I fended off with my right hand, leaning into the rock wall, but the boat struck. The impact tore the fabric of the hull where it was backed by the gunwale stringer, but I considered the damage unimportant because the water that could come through this hole was small compared to the amount that poured over the cockpit coaming in every rapid.

This was a section of river with powerful eddy currents below the drops. Once I swung into an eddy and found that the upstream current against the bank was so swift I couldn't land without getting into an eddy within the eddy. First I had to make an eddy-turn upstream and then downstream. There were often whirlpools along the eddy lines. It was easy to avoid them, but after each whirlpool there was an upwelling of water that moved unpredictably across the surface. Several times these mounds of water thumped the bottom of my boat, knocking it sideways.

Shortly after encountering the whirlpools, I felt a gust of warm, dry air in my face. This was very different from the cool air I had experienced for all of my trip. The gusts were intermittent and for a while puzzled me. Then I reasoned that a hot wind was blowing in the canyon of the Main Salmon and an eddy of this wind was pushing up into the canyon of the Middle Fork. The junction could not be far ahead. Shortly I had better proof. After a jog in the direction of the river, I found myself looking down a mile-long dark corridor of canyon toward a sunlit wall that seemed to block the far end. At the foot of the wall, and just above water level, there was a row of evenly spaced objects. I didn't know what they were, but from their regularity I knew that they must be manmade and therefore on the far bank of the Main Salmon, the first spot accessible by road since the bridge over Marsh Creek. I ran that last mile without scouting or even pausing for the few remaining rapids. When I beached my boat on the left bank, where the Middle Fork emptied into the Main Salmon, it was with a great feeling of relief. I had traveled 112 miles and dropped 3,500 feet, all in a bit over seven days. I knew I would run rivers again, but for now I would run not one more mile nor drop one more foot through whitewater.

11

River's End

When I climbed out of the cockpit and heaved the boat up on shore, I looked down and saw, in a patch of damp sand, footprints such as I'd seen at the falls and at two of the landslide rapids on the upper river. In the past few days, I had forgotten about Hindman and my original plan to catch up to him. Now that the trip was over, I was glad that I had made it down the entire river alone.

As I looked about me, I realized that this place, the junction of two rivers, was an appropriate end to the Middle Fork. This new canyon, the canyon of the Main Salmon, was very different. It was larger, more open, more full of light. A hot wind, the same that had sent eddies up into the canyon of the Middle Fork, was blowing through the canyon of the Main Salmon. It was an upstream wind, a phenomenon all too familiar to river

runners. Here the two rivers met at right angles, the Middle
Fork from the south intersecting the Main Salmon which
flowed from east to west. The water of the Middle Fork was
clear, but the Main Salmon was muddy, the result of mining
operations on a tributary far upstream. The clear water and the
muddy water came together but didn't mingle immediately.
Clear and muddy ran side by side with a sharp if undulating
boundary between them. A hundred yards downstream, the
two rivers began to meld. Perhaps some of the waters coming
together had originated in the marsh where Stu's car had stuck
in the mud. That marsh drained in two directions, to the west
into the Middle Fork which cut through the Salmon River
Mountains, and to the east into the Main Salmon which took an
easier and longer route, passing through broader valleys and
by mining towns and ranching centers, and all the way paralleled by a road. The road was just across the Main Salmon from
where I stood, and I could now see that the evenly spaced objects were lengths of pine logs, placed beside the road as a
guardrail. The road was deserted, but I would have to find
someone to give me a ride for the fifty miles to Salmon City,
where I could catch the stage, as the bus was called, to Sun Valley. But first, I must pay my respects to Gus Peebles, who lived
in a cabin a short distance from where I had landed.

I knocked at the door of the cabin and immediately heard a
high-pitched, excited barking. The door was opened by an
elderly man dressed in a gray wool shirt and corduroy knick-
ers. He had a full head of white hair that must have been
cropped under a bowl. He looked at me in silence. A small
black and white dog growled at me from a safe position behind
the man's heels.

"Mr. Peebles?"

"Yes."

"I've just come down the Middle Fork alone . . . "

"The hell you say! Come right in. You look hungry. Have you
had anything to eat?"

"Well, no."

"Then I'll fix you supper."

As I stepped into the cabin, there was more barking from the dog.

"Quiet there, King Zog, quiet!" Gus shouted. Then in explanation, "That there dog is named King Zog, after the King of Albania." I knew about King Zog, a deposed monarch whose name and adventures popped up in the newspapers from time to time, giving some relief to the usual dismal war reports. Gus continued. "That dog, when he was just a puppy, peed on Ernest Hemingway's son. That makes him kind of a famous dog."

"I expect so," I agreed, then asked, "When did Hindman and his party come through, Mr. Peebles?"

"Yesterday," he said. "They had a good ride. The first time they'd run it in high water, but they said that's the way to do it. Somebody wasn't so lucky though; drowned up near the beginning of the river. Hindman found his sleeping bag with his name on it. Fellow named Friedman. Was he with you?"

"Yes, he lost his boat and all his duffle, including his sleeping bag, but he didn't drown; he got ashore OK."

"Well, I'm glad to hear that," said Gus Peebles.

"Mr. Peebles," I asked, "do you remember Zee Grant who ran the Middle Fork two years ago?"

"Sure I remember him. Now there was a great fellow. He a friend of yours?"

"Yes."

"Well, sit down here and tell me about how he's doing and about how you came down the river. My, my! Do you know there's hundreds of prospectors in the West who would give their eye teeth to get into that canyon you just come through."

As with everything else in the cabin, the table was incredibly cluttered, but Gus cleared a space in front of me and then heaped my plate with potatoes and beans. I wolfed down the food and then, feeling that my appetite needed an explanation, I recounted my experience with the spruce grouse.

"How should I have cooked it?" I asked.

Gus snorted. "Your spruce grouse is very tough in the winter and spring when all he gets to eat is spruce needles and maybe some nuts and seeds. Later on, he eats grasshoppers and gets very plump and tender, but this time of year, the best you can do is boil him for three hours in an iron pot, then throw away the bird and eat the pot."

I laughed and kept on eating. Gus talked without stopping, telling a remarkable jumble of stories, things that had happened a few days before, mixed with events long past. He had been a salt-water sailor and then a river-boat captain on the Yukon in the gold rush days. I was too drained to listen carefully, but I was grateful to receive his hospitality, to be out of the canyon of the Middle Fork, and to be at the end of the hazardous portion of my adventure, if not quite back in the modern world of 1942.

In the next step of my journey, Gus was of great help. He knew a young man who had driven down from a town named North River and who was fishing somewhere on the opposite bank. While I folded my boat, Gus crossed the Main Salmon on a small, hand-pulled cable car. He located the fisherman and found that, for a price, the driver was willing to take me to Salmon City. Gus, King Zog, the fisherman, and I made the long trip on a dirt road that closely paralleled the river. Most of the trip was in the dark, and as we drove, our headlights picked out an astonishing number of deer. Gus said they liked to feel the flat surface of the road. In that canyon and beside the river there was very little else that was horizontal. The fisherman packed a big automatic in a belt holster and had a rifle in the car as well. He hinted that he would like to pick off one of the deer, and I hinted just as strongly that I had no wish to be party to jacking a deer, and out of season, too. I was paying good money for the ride, so caution prevailed, but when a huge porcupine blundered into the road ahead of us, the fisherman had a chance to vent his frustration. He jammed on the brakes, leapt out of the car, and blazed away with his automatic. The porcupine escaped over the bank and among the rocks that lined the river. I hoped none of the bullets found the small body inside the larger target provided by the quills. At Salmon, we stopped at the hotel and I took leave of Gus, King Zog, and the fisherman. When I registered, the clerk asked if I wanted a room for a dollar fifty with a window or for a dollar without. In those days, Salmon City was not a fancy place.

Next morning, I sent a telegram to my parents and then climbed on the stage, the small bus that traveled north one day and south the next. For most of the distance we traveled on a dirt road, almost empty of traffic. The bus driver waved to almost every car or truck that we did pass. Idaho was like a small town in which everyone knows everyone else. I chatted with the driver, and when we reached Shotgun Rapid he stopped so that I could have a look at the drop. This was the rapid that Zee had run in 1938. Not long after leaving Shotgun, we came to Stanley and stopped at the gas station, where I dropped off the inner tubes that Slim had lent me. The station owner said he'd give them to Slim. Then we drove through Stanley Basin, up over Galena Summit, now dry of snow, and down into the Wood River drainage. At Sun Valley I got off the bus with my boat and duffle bag and I said good-by to the driver.

When I walked in the door of the Challenger Inn, the dark-haired girl behind the reception desk looked up with a startled expression.

"You're supposed to be dead," she said.

"Well, I'm not. I'm very much alive," I answered. Not a clever line, but how often does one think of a clever line in real life?

"I think Taylor Williams will want to talk to you," said the girl.

Soon I was talking to Taylor Williams and then to the public relations man, who sent off a story on the wire service. Next day my friends read in the eastern papers that I had survived, which says much for the novelty of whitewater boating in 1942.

I sought out the staff doctor to look at my still swollen and oozing leg. He bandaged the wound and told me not to worry about it, and he didn't charge me anything. Next, I chanced to meet the ski instructor who had recommended that I try a Sun Valley "pioneer cabin." He was still wearing his ski boots and was still very condescending.

"You worried your mother; you shouldn't have done that." It was obvious that my mother's telegram was common knowledge at Sun Valley. Well, it was their slow season; with the place nearly empty, they needed something to talk about.

"You're absolutely right," I said, no longer annoyed by this man, but amused by his need to appear superior.

Two days later I was on the eastbound train, sitting beside an attractive ballet dancer who lived on Long Island. I had come full circle; I had made the transition back to my own familiar world. The Middle Fork was receding into the past, but at the same time it was still with me. I was on my way home, not just after an exciting vacation adventure, a hare-brained enterprise, somehow survived, but after a rite of passage, a loss of innocence. I was changed. I knew that the experience might not convey wisdom in all matters, nor bravery at all times, nor guarantee any other virtue, but it would make a difference for as long as I lived.

Back East and in college, I was soon in touch with Ed, Stu, and Zee. Stu sent me a letter beginning, "You old son of a gun! Congratulations on making it through to the Salmon." It was fall before I was able to get together with Ed and fill him in on what happened to me after he had seen me disappear down Marsh Creek. To Zee, I sent a detailed account of the trip, which he shared with his friends on the Amorita.

Three years later while on leave from the Marine Corps, I teamed up with Zee for a river trip. We took our foldboats by train to Calicoon and floated down the Delaware to Lackawaxen, a run that included only one drop that I can remember, Skinner's Falls. We made a two-day trip of it. At the end of the first day, we faced such a strong upstream wind that we couldn't force our boats downriver. We beached our boats and walked two miles to the inn where we were to spend the night. Zee was a diabetic; this hadn't stopped him from running the Green, the Middle Fork, and the Grand Canyon of the Colorado, but on this occasion the exertion of paddling and of walking against the cold wind drained the blood sugar from his system. I insisted on carrying his duffle bag as well as mine, but Zee was in poor shape when we reached the inn. We sat in the warmth of the barroom, watching old men play a form of shuffleboard on a long table. Zee asked for orange juice. That wasn't available, so he revived himself with a daiquiri. Then we ate dinner. Zee was as cheerful as ever and talked about adventures he was planning for the future, but I doubted that there would be any expeditions on the rivers that flow down out of the Himalaya.

Zee did very little boating after 1945, but he led an active life. He married; he and his wife Margaret had a daughter named Sarah. Zee's health continued to deteriorate. In 1966 he wrote for the Harvard alumni notes, "Since last report, I have done little but get very sick and then very well again. Working for an airline, I have traveled quite a bit, but mostly I mow the lawn and otherwise tend my little place in the country." He died in 1971.

In my own future there was a good deal of whitewater, though no more solo plunges down wilderness rivers. After the war, which to my surprise didn't last for twenty years, I found a job in the Boston area and simultaneously found the Appalachian Mountain Club whitewater canoeing program. In this group was a girl named Barbara Rowe, who held the distinction of having been in the bow of the first Grumman aluminum canoe wrapped around a rock. The fault was clearly with the fellow in the stern; she needed a better stern paddler. For that as well as other reasons, we married. For years we spent every weekend in the spring running New England rivers. We would begin in March, often with snow on the ground, on rivers in Connecticut, Massachusetts, or lower New Hampshire. Mid-April would find us on the West River in Vermont. Later we would run the Saco and the Ammonoosuc. Much of what we ran was rocky and steep, technically demanding but not big water. The one river that reminded me a bit of the Middle Fork was the upper Hudson, a tough, turbulent river flowing through a gorge. Still, running any river is a joy, a celebration of the immediate.

For a few years, our group ran rivers as if we were the only people in the world with this particular enthusiasm. We never saw other boats on our rivers or on the tops of cars on roads leading into the river country. There seemed to be even fewer people enjoying whitewater sports than in the prewar period. We knew of a few other canoeists: Appalachian Mountain Club groups based in Connecticut and New York, the Buck Ridge Ski Club in Pennsylvania. Occasionally we held joint trips with these other groups. In a few years, the number of participants in our own program grew, and we found that we were training canoeists who went on to establish whitewater programs in other outing clubs. The Buck Ridge Ski Club was even more active in its training program. It was a luxury to have had the rivers to ourselves, but that condition was not consistent with the changing postwar scene.

A new generation was discovering the mountains and rivers of America. Beginning in the late 1940s, there was an astonishing increase in the number of people participating in wilderness recreation. No doubt there were sociological reasons for this rush to the backcountry, but for me, the physical and technological reasons are more easily understood. Improved roads provided quick access to recreational areas. Army-surplus camping gear was inexpensive and serviceable, if not as elegant as today's refined equipment. The new aluminum canoes were much more durable than the old canvas-on-wood models, and it was easier to train newcomers in a fleet of uniform boats than in a heterogeneous assemblage of broken-bottomed wooden hulls. For the kayaker, first there came greatly improved foldboats from Europe; then came fiberglass, allowing the construction of lighter and more durable hulls. These first fiberglass kayaks were home designed and home built and were therefore relatively inexpensive. For people who preferred to run rivers in oared boats, navy-surplus rafts provided a cheap access to rivers. Later came more exotic materials, improvements in design, and a switch from surplus or homemade equipment to equipment manufactured specifically for the whitewater market, but the general trend was to make river running more available to the public.

Other factors contributed to the increased popularity of whitewater. One was the introduction of whitewater slalom, a form of competition derived from ski slalom. The gates, each consisting of two poles, are suspended from cables that span the river. Competitors race against the clock, but if a pole is touched, that adds ten seconds to the time. Gates are placed so as to force the contestants into the most difficult water, to make quick turns in and out of eddies, to slide across the main current, and even to sprint upstream for short distances.

Organized whitewater slalom began in the United States in April of 1953 with a race put on by the Buck Ridge Ski Club. The objects were to add variety to the standard river-running schedule and to improve boating skills. Judging from letters, photographs, and printed materials received by American boaters, the Europeans were ahead of us in technique. Their skills appeared to have been developed largely through slalom. The first races in this country were modest affairs, on easy water, with participants coming from only a few clubs. Very soon, races were held on more demanding water, and there developed a cadre of enthusiastic young people who would travel any distance for the opportunity to charge through a series of gates in a kayak or a canoe. Skill levels improved noticeably.

Another factor contributing to improved boating skill was

the direct help that Americans received from European boaters. A number of experts came to this country temporarily or settled here permanently. One was Eric Seidel, from Germany. He was an early winner of a downriver race held on the Arkansas River at Salida, Colorado. Seidel set up the first demonstration slalom in Colorado. Walter Kierchbaum, also from Germany, showed American kayakers that it was possible to run drops that they had considered unrunnable. In 1960 he ran the Grand Canyon. He was the next kayaker to make the trip after Zee Grant's 1941 run. Zee had carried around Lava Falls, a Class V rapid, but Kierchbaum ran it. Rogere Paris, of France, was another early winner at Salida. He and his wife Jackie stayed on in America. They joined the faculty of the Colorado Rocky Mountain School and contributed to the training of a whole generation of American boaters.

Another European who substantially helped us was Milo Duffek. Milo, a native of Czechoslovakia, competed internationally as a member of the Czech team. Then he defected to Switzerland and competed on the Swiss team. Originally a canoeist, he switched to kayak, adapting canoe strokes to kayak handling. On his forward strokes, his paddle shaft was absolutely vertical; his paddle brace was incredibly stable. "Duffek turn" became a part of whitewater language.

In 1964, Milo and wife Irmgard came to America to conduct a series of on-river training sessions. The first of these sessions was on the Rapid River in Maine, scene of the prewar national championships. With my older son Kin, I participated in this session. Milo was a patient and inspiring teacher, but the high point for me was running through the big pitches of the Rapid River immediately behind Milo. It had been twenty-three years since I'd been through those rapids. That run was a nostalgic experience, and at the same time an opportunity to observe a master river runner in his element and to consider the advances that were taking place in whitewater boating.

For a person approaching middle age and having demanding

career commitments, keeping up with all the new develop-
ments wasn't easy. I learned to handle the newer kayaks, but
not with the proficiency I would have liked. I dutifully prac-
ticed my Eskimo roll, but my long-conditioned reaction, when
upside down in whitewater under a boat, was to bail out, just
as I had done on the Middle Fork. In slalom, Barbara and I competed in our canoe, and I competed in single foldboat. I had one
moment of triumph. In 1958, on the West River in Vermont, I
won the national championship. I beat a number of younger
boaters who had boats of more advanced design but who
hadn't yet learned how to use them. By the next year, the tables
were turned.

I was able to participate in the coming of age of whitewater
boating in another way. In the early fifties, I joined forces with
Bob McNair of the Buck Ridge Ski Club to form a nationwide
organization of whitewater boaters. This was a revival of Zee's
attempt to form a River Rats of America. But because Bob and I
believed that the sport was best carried out by clubs, or at least
by informal groups of boaters, we named the organization the
American Whitewater Affiliation. At the start we emphasized
club membership, but soon this was supplemented by an individual membership list. The AWA began publishing a journal,
American Whitewater, in 1955. A safety code soon followed. In
the 1959 version of the code, rule number one was, "Never boat
alone; the preferred minimum is three craft." That was a rule I
could sincerely endorse, more because of than in spite of my
solo run down the Middle Fork.

As Barbara and I dropped out of our direct involvement in
whitewater boating, the sport gained in popularity beyond our
wildest expectations. Rivers that had seldom if ever been disturbed by a paddle became crowded by weekend kayakers and
canoeists. The big western rivers received a flood of rafts, operated by both professional and private boaters. American teams
competed successfully in international slalom, even winning
top honors at the world championships held in 1979 at

Jonquiere, Quebec. Whitewater guidebooks and books on technique became standard items on the bookshelves of sporting-goods stores. We kept track of all of this through reading *American Whitewater*, through our two sons Kin and Del, both whitewater boatmen, and through the ever-increasing media coverage of the sport.

Through all this time interval, the Middle Fork, like a friend of early years, was somewhere in the back of my mind. I wondered what had become of the river. Had it survived the impact of the whitewater boating explosion? I kept a file on the Middle Fork, including my old notes, letters, telegrams, and maps. To this I added articles I clipped from magazines over the years. From time to time, there was an article or a note referring to the river in *American Whitewater*. I had a few closer contacts with the river. In 1968, the family having moved to California, Barbara, Kin, Del, and I took a backpacking vacation in the Sawtooth Mountains. We drove on the new road to Dagger Falls, where I identified the rock by which I had built my fire twenty-six years earlier. Ten years later, in 1978, Del kayaked the Middle Fork with a group of his friends. He and I talked a good deal about his trip. From all these sources I was able to form a general impression of what was happening to the river.

12

The Breath of Life

Boatmen were back on the river shortly after World War II. Russell Frazier made a trip in 1945 and in the course of that trip gave a short ride to an Idaho man named Leon Anderson. Anderson was immediately hooked on whitewater. He bought a surplus raft and with his brother went into the river-guide business. Leon's son Ted eventually became a forest service river manager, with responsibilities for the Middle Fork and the Main Salmon rivers. Hindman and his partner Prince Helfrich were back on the Middle Fork in 1946. Prince Helfrich's son eventually carried on the business. Hatch River Expeditions, a firm founded by Bus Hatch and his son Don, started taking people down the river. The Hatches, in addition to taking passengers on their rafts, also acted as escort to groups of kayakers. In this system the raft carries all food and camping gear, allowing the kayakers the greater freedom that comes from paddling unloaded boats.

At first the river use was relatively light. This was because parties running the river had either to launch on Bear Valley Creek or pack in to some lower section of the river. Then, in 1959, the Forest Service extended the Bear Valley road to Dagger Falls and to Boundary Creek. The purpose of this extension was to allow the hauling of cement and other materials for the construction of a fish ladder around Dagger Falls. The salmon, already thwarted by dams farther downstream in the Columbia River system, were to be given easier access to their spawning beds in the Middle Fork headwaters. Quite aside from what this development did for the salmon, it was a boon for commercial river runners. They could now avoid the punishing rocks of Bear Valley Creek and the first ten miles of the Middle Fork. Some of the challenge faced by early boaters had been lost, but there was quicker access to the big water downstream. All the ingredients that could contribute to the expansion of river traffic were present but, like yeast in bread dough, needed time.

One important component of the recipe was publicity. Guides advertised their services, but in addition to that, articles about the Middle Fork, as well as other big western rivers, appeared in newspapers and magazines. The authors of these articles tried to strike a balance between emphasizing the excitement of running the river and the competence of the guides. They were selling hazard and safety at the same time. However difficult that may sound, it worked. A float trip down a major river became a reasonable vacation option for the general public. In addition, the amateur boaters, increasing in number and competence year by year, looked to the wilderness rivers for their vacation adventures. The boom was on; the Middle Fork became one of the popular whitewater rivers. By 1967, the annual use of the river, by professional boatmen, their passengers, and by amateurs, was at the two thousand level and increasing at the rate of five hundred per year.

With increased use of the river there came problems. There was friction between various professional outfitters, particularly between guides from different regions. Some Idaho guides felt they should have the exclusive right to take parties down a river that from start to finish was in their state. There was also some friction between professionals and amateurs. The first days of the week were the most popular for starting downriver. This resulted in traffic jams and frayed tempers at the launch site, with vehicles backed up a mile waiting to put in. On the river, there were certain preferred campsites. Numerous parties crowded into these areas at the same time. With the accumulation of trash and human waste, such places became unsightly and unsanitary. It was customary for boaters to bury their trash in certain pits and just as customary for bears to dig up and scatter the refuse. Yellowjackets and other insects fed on the trash piles. Fire rings with piles of ashes dotted the ground at these favored camping spots. Except for the bears, there was a reduction in wildlife. The cutthroat trout, for which the river had been famous, were overfished and started to disappear. The values that attracted people to the river were being destroyed by the people.

There was a problem of safety. There was little or no regulation of who could run the river, no check on equipment, no restraint about running the river at high water. In June of 1970, at flood stage, three men drowned in the Middle Fork, one near Sulfur Creek and the other two after an upset in Weber Rapid, the same drop that had nearly finished me. The first accident was to a private group, the second to a party under the command of an experienced professional river guide. That accident, in which one boatman and one passenger died, received a great deal of publicity because newsman Tom Brokaw was one of the survivors.

The inevitable consequence of these problems was that the National Forest Service took direct control of the river. For years the Forest Service had had a general responsibility for the river, but in 1968 they were handed a special responsibility because the Middle Fork was one of the rivers included in the Wild and Scenic Rivers Act.

The first step taken by the Forest Service was to study the physical condition of the river and its surroundings, taking note of the river use, the condition of the campgrounds, and of a vast number of other factors. The study's findings were published in January, 1973 in a document entitled "Recreation Management Plan, Middle Fork Salmon Wild and Scenic River."

Under the plan, river runners could no longer start down the river at will. They had to apply to the Forest Service and receive starting dates. A general division of river use was made between professional and private trips. Three starts were allowed by professional parties per day, and four by private parties, but because the regulations allowed more people in a professional than in a private party, there resulted a 70 percent to 30 percent professional versus private split of river use. The professionals allowed to run the river were the ones who were already using it; they were "grandfathered" into a franchise system. Private river runners were either given starting dates or rejected on the basis of a sort of computer lottery. The objects of these regulations were to put a limit on river use and to distribute river use evenly over the summer season, a season usually defined by the end of the flood stage in middle to late June to low water, too low for practical boating, in early September.

Steps were also taken to distribute boaters along the river. Each party was scheduled into its own campsite each night while on the river, the professional groups being assigned to the larger campgrounds, and the private groups usually being assigned to smaller sites. Trip leaders were given a voice in the selection of these campgrounds, but the expectation was that they would keep to their schedules except in an emergency. In addition, the Forest Service laid down the law on camping practices. There were to be no more garbage pits; all trash was to be carried out. Fires were to be built only in metal fire pans, each party carrying its own pan, and then the ashes were to be packed in plastic bags and carried out. Although there were open-air privies at at least a third of the campgrounds, boaters had the responsibility of carrying out all human waste when stopping at the other campgrounds.

There were a number of other changes: The Forest Service made certain safety regulations with regard to equipment, and it required professional outfitters to be adequately covered by insurance. The state of Idaho had licensing requirements for professional guides. The Idaho Fish and Wildlife Service decreed that all fishing in the river must be with barbless hooks and that all trout must be released. The purpose of this was to save the cutthroat trout population.

The Forest Service, in addition to imposing these and other regulations, took a number of steps for the convenience of boaters. They built an impressive launch-site complex at Boundary Creek and a take-out ramp with parking lot, rest rooms, and trash bins at the end of the run. To enhance the wilderness character of the river, they made some changes in the trail system along its banks and burned some of the old mining cabins.

It was a big change; some might say it was the heavy hand of Big Brother. The controls went into effect in 1973. Boaters who had been using the river without any restraint now grumbled and fretted under a system of regulation. In time, most accepted the system, realizing that as river use approached a ceiling of eight thousand, the alternative to control was chaos.

Would it be safe to conclude that the river and its eight thousand travelers represent an idyllic marriage of the modern world and the wilderness? Can we say that they lived happily ever after once mother-in-law Forest Service imposed some rules on the marriage? Hardly. The pressures that put eight thousand people on the river are still at work and are felt in a number of ways.

Consider the private boaters. There are now at least a quarter-million whitewater kayakers, rafters, and canoeists in the United States. Of these, perhaps twenty-five thousand are truly dedicated and spend much of their free time running rivers. These people do most of their boating on short sections of river that are close to home. Some of these rivers are beautiful, and some are technically difficult, but few of them take the boater very far from roads. Many of these rivers are crowded with canoes and rafts. I have heard one Colorado river described as a zoo. No wonder that to weekend boaters there is something infinitely attractive about a vacation trip down a wilderness river. They want to leave the crowds and the roads behind. They want to float a river by day and camp on the bank each night. The Middle Fork offers an attractive and not too remote option for such an experience.

Not only do the boaters want to run rivers such as the Middle Fork, they feel it's their right to run such rivers. The great whitewater rivers of America are a repertoire which serious boaters feel they have a right to experience. They believe that if a boater has invested the effort necessary to become competent enough to run the Middle Fork, he or she should be allowed to do so. This feeling is thwarted by the necessity of submitting to a quota system, however benign in intent, that gives a private boater only about a 20 percent chance of getting a starting date on the Middle Fork. The frustration is increased by the knowledge that a passenger on a professional trip earns the right to run the river merely by plunking down the necessary money. It is possible to argue that the professional guides have a long history of use of the river and that their passengers represent a public that has a right to enjoy the public wilderness. The passenger may not be capable of dodging rocks and souse holes but may perhaps have an equal or greater appreciation of the scenic values, the geology, the wildlife, the history—all valid components of the wilderness experience.

Limited access is not unique to the Middle Fork. There are at least twelve big western rivers or sections of rivers that are similarly managed. For some rivers, getting a permit is more likely than for the Middle Fork, but for others it is less likely. Receiving a permit to run the Grand Canyon of the Colorado may take years. It is difficult to receive a permit for the Selway because only one party is allowed down that river per day, and the majority are professional parties. Still, a boater who applies for most of the controlled rivers has a good chance of acceptance for at least one of the runs. It is also possible to show up at the launch site and wait on a stand-by basis for a cancellation or for a small group that is willing to expand its number, provided that the total number falls within the maximum allowed. Other boaters gain access to controlled rivers by running them out of season, when there is little competition for starting dates. Some kayakers run the Middle Fork in April or May, catching the river before the peak floods. Because the road to Bear Valley and Boundary Creek is usually impassable at that season, they start down Marsh Creek, as I did. That's a risky business because the creek can be blocked by avalanches of snow that have swept down the steep canyon wall. There is also risk because a thaw may drastically increase the volume of water in the river when the party is halfway down.

A few boaters out-and-out defy the authorities. They make unauthorized runs down the big rivers. Sometimes they are caught and fined and sometimes they get away with it. Many other boaters don't participate in such trips but still applaud them as a form of protest. They perceive the villain to be the government. Perhaps the regulations could be bent more in favor of the private boater, but the real problem is that whitewater rivers are a limited resource.

Professionals are also at a disadvantage. The operator of a rafting company can't expand without buying out another franchise, finding a new river, or putting pressure on the government to modify its rules. Franchises are not often up for sale, and when they are, the prices can be astonishingly high. The new rivers are in Alaska, Canada, or South America, and there are boating companies that specialize in running rivers all over the globe. Putting pressure on the government, either to enlarge the size of parties or the number of parties, or to squeeze out the private parties, is tried from time to time, but the Forest Service, National Park Service, and the Bureau of Land Management have a tendency to maintain the status quo. For the most part, the company operator is locked into his existing business. That may be frustrating, but for the individual professional boatman, the situation is worse. He has virtually no chance to strike out and start his own company.

All of the conflicts between boaters and the government and between the different segments of the boating population are of minor importance when compared to external threats. How the Middle Fork can accommodate its friends is less of a concern than how it can survive its enemies. The concept of leaving a river in its natural condition is in direct conflict with the demand for irrigation, for electric power, and for flood control. Wherever there is a flowing river at a higher altitude than potential farmland, there is political pressure to divert water to irrigation projects. Wherever water runs downhill, there is political pressure for the construction of power dams. Wherever people have built on a flood plain, there is political pressure to build flood-control dams upstream. In each case, a supporting argument is made on the basis of the jobs created in building the dam and the recreational value of power boating and fishing on a new lake. The counter arguments—that new farmland only adds to the existing surplus, that consumption of electricity could be reduced, that it is foolish to build on a flood plain—those arguments are abstruse and have little appeal to the local voter. The political pressure is relentless. Rivers are lost one by one. In 1947 and again in 1949, Barbara and I canoed a fantastic whitewater section of Vermont's West River. ·A few years later, the best of it was obliterated by the Ball Mountain Dam. It happens again and again.

Compared to rivers over which conservationists and developers are now battling tooth and nail, the Middle Fork is safe. "Wild and Scenic" designation provides security, but that security is relative. What the Congress has done, Congress can undo. Within recent years there has been a move to modify the act to allow individual states to reduce protection of a river flowing entirely within that state's boundaries. I don't know if there were specific designs on the Middle Fork, but anyone who has studied the topo maps of the area can see that it would be relatively easy to divert waters from the headwaters of the river to agricultural lands in southern Idaho. The 1932 map even shows where to put the dam. The map may be out of print but no doubt the Army Corps of Engineers has copies on file. As population in the West increases, there will be greater demands for water and power. Farms, homes, manufacturing plants, and cities will be an influence to change, if not completely destroy, the river.

Even if the Middle Fork is left with all of its federal protection, it can be damaged at a distance, shot down on the wing by forces of the modern world. One threat is presented by acid rain, which is particularly damaging in regions where the underlying rock is impervious and insoluble, as with the metamorphic and granitic rock of the Middle Fork drainage. Another threat comes from the "greenhouse effect." Carbon dioxide, released into the atmosphere by the burning of fossil fuels, traps solar energy. Many scientists believe that this process is slowly modifying world climate and that, in the not too distant future, the western United States will be hotter and dryer. If this is true, then forests, rivers, wildlife, and indeed the entire ecosystem will suffer.

In the long run, the very long run, the river will survive. Rivers are among the most enduring features of the landscape, often much older than mountains or canyons through which they flow. The present condition of the Middle Fork as a deeply canyoned river may be just one phase of a cycle that continually changes the landscape, and in which uplift and erosion alternate as the dominant process. I picture the Middle Fork at some distant time in the past. It flows through a broad valley. Dinosaurs drink at the bank, and in the water, swimming upstream to spawn, are the ancestors of the present-day salmon. Perhaps a volcano on the horizon presages a time when the land under the river will push up into mountains and the river will cut down to form a canyon. I also picture the Middle Fork in the future, again in a broad valley, the mountains having been eroded away, but what living things are on its banks or in its waters I can't imagine. Perhaps it's best to deal with the Middle Fork in the present.

In June of 1981, while I was lying in my hospital bed after a major operation for cancer, my thoughts went back to my adventure of 1942. I began to relive the experience in my imagination and at the same time tried to relate that experience to the modern world. I realized that I was approaching the fortieth anniversary of my descent of the river and that forty years is a period that has a special Biblical significance. Forty years, and also forty days, are periods of healing, of insight, of return. I hoped for healing and insight, but I didn't expect return, except in imagination. Then, the next winter, when our son Del was visiting us, he asked, "How would you like to go down the Middle Fork next summer?"

How would I like to breathe the breath of life?

Pistol Creek Rapid on the Middle Fork, August 1982

August 26, 1982

Take-out Point

We were on the river. Barbara and I were in the front of Del's raft. Cisco, in his big, black cowboy hat, piloted his raft—the Francesca. His passengers were Mardi and Dottie. Jayne and Eric were in another raft. The fourth raft was piloted by Mark, with Rene as his passenger.

I was astonished at the number of people running the river. We were seldom out of sight of other rafts, not just the rafts of our party, but rafts of other parties. Perhaps we saw more because we got a late start and had a long way to go to our assigned campground. Del pushed ahead, passing rafts that were just drifting with the current. The traffic was densest at the big drops. Just above Sulfur Slide and again at Velvet Falls there were rows of rafts tied up to the bank, and a well-worn path led downstream to where people stood on the bank or sat on rocks picking their own routes and watching other boatmen come through one by one. At Velvet a young man just barely got his raft lined up for the slot, which is river-left.

"Did you see that?" asked Mark. "He was out of control."

I nodded, remembering that I had been swept over these falls dead center.

At the next big rapid, The Chutes, there was a scene of confusion. A raft of one of the other parties had become wrapped around a rock. A rope had been thrown to the raft from the right bank and the rescue operation was under way. There were enough people on the scene, so we didn't stop. As we slid by on the opposite side of the rock from the rope, we saw that one of the men involved in getting the raft off the rock was without a life jacket. Del called out, "Put on your life jacket." The man followed Del's advice. We noted that this raft belonged to a group that was negligent about wearing life jackets. Perhaps they thought it unnecessary because the water was low. That is foolish. If you develop the habit of going without a life jacket, then you will extend the habit into more and more hazardous water, and eventually you will get into trouble. Later we learned that the Forest Service can require every boater to have a life jacket, but wearing the life jacket is a personal or group option. If a professional outfitter shows laxness in safety, the Forest Service has some leverage, but not so with a private group.

The crowd at The Chutes had held back the traffic and we had the river mostly to ourselves. As we approached Powerhouse Rapid, the longest rapid on the upper river, I looked for it, using the same landmarks I had used in 1942. Everything was the same. As we slammed through without scouting, I was able to describe to Del what was coming up next.

We camped at a place known as Fire Island. I was impressed by the cleanliness of the site. There was no trash, no fire circles with ashes, only a few worn places on the ground. The Forest Service rules appeared to work. In the morning, the Forest Service sweep raft stopped by. Three young employees were checking all campgrounds on their way downriver. We had an agreeable chat with them. They left and we followed shortly after. Again, we were in the company of other rafts.

On this, our second day, I was particularly anxious to identify the place where my shivering spell had made it so difficult for me to scout a bad chute. The modern guidebooks don't describe such a spot a mile below Rapid River. When we had gone that mile, the place clicked in my memory. The configuration of the canyon, with the big slide-rock slope on the left, was unchanged. The trunks of two dead trees pushed up out of a gravel bar. Could these be the same dead trees by which I had built my fire forty years earlier? The trunks were worn from withstanding the impact of debris carried along by floodwater. I was sure they were the same trees. Although the current was swift here, the big rapid was gone. There was no impoundment of water, no narrow chute through the rock dam. Erosion had changed the river, but the spot was unmistakable.

Pistol Creek, where I had escaped being swept into a log, came next. Here again, I recognized every feature of the rapid. The eddy where I had sought refuge was still there; Mark slipped his raft into this same eddy to avoid collision with a raft from another party. The narrow chute down which I had taken my kayak was still there, though at this stage only a trickle of water dropped through it. From the bank I watched as raft after raft ran the S-turn. Two rafts bumped into each other in the middle of the drop.

We stopped for lunch a short distance downstream, just below the spot where Pistol Creek came in on the left. Mardi spread a plastic sheet on the ground and then set out crackers, cheese, peanut butter, kippered herring in a can. Rene brought cans of beer. It was like a picnic lunch in an urban park, and just as populated. There were people swimming in the river below the drop, people walking in the woods beside the river, people starting out again on their rafts to drift downstream.

Still, it was a delightful setting. The air was full of small, white butterflies with delicate dark brown markings tracing the edges of their wings.

We got back in the rafts and started downstream. We passed a row of vacation cottages on the left bank. They were on a piece of private property, called an "inholding," within the National Forest. There was an airstrip in back of the cottages. The owners of these cabins could fly here, or be piloted here by air-taxi for a weekend of fishing or just sitting on the terrace with a drink in hand, watching the parade of rafts. The last cottage, a splendid A-frame, was for sale. Barbara wanted to write down the telephone number of the realtor, but I said, "Don't bother. The price would be out of sight."

A few miles farther on, I looked for Pungo Creek. We spotted it on the left and Del swung into shore. Barbara and I climbed up through a thick stand of ponderosa pine to the remains of Ed Budell's cabin—not much left but a few logs on a level piece of ground. We took pictures. A boatman from one of the other parties came up. We talked; I explained that I had spent the night in this cabin forty years earlier. He wanted to know why I was running the river in '42. Was it for some commercial reason, or just for fun? "Just for fun," I said.

Barbara and I went back to the raft. Del was impatient to move on as the other rafts in our party had passed us. He pushed ahead, alternating strokes with the right and left oars, but still facing downstream. We found that the others had already stopped at our next campground, called Lonesome Oak, a short distance below Marble Creek. This campground was on a high bluff above the river. There was a nice view downstream.

Next day I did most of the rowing, with Del coaching me. This was the middle portion of the river where the rapids were not so severe. Still, there were rocks to be dodged. For the most part, I drifted with the raft at right angles to the current, rowing forward or back to stay in the best channel. Del, sitting just behind me on the pile of duffle, explained that in New Mexico, where he is a professional river guide, the two questions most frequently asked by clients are: "How deep is the river?" and "Why are we going sideways?"The first question is difficult to answer because the depth of a whitewater river changes constantly. As for the second question, the raft is rowed across current so as to reach water that is headed between, not into, the next set of obstacles. When you reach a narrow place, or a drop, or a series of waves, a push on one oar or a tug on the other will straighten out the raft in the current. Del showed me how, when negotiating a rapid at a bend of the river, you start at the outside of the bend and row toward the inside, building up momentum so that the raft slides past the large rocks and waves on the outside and rides the quieter water close to the eddy line. In a kayak or canoe, I would have kept to the inside for the whole route, but a raft has its own rules. It is heavy. The essence of handling it is to make its momentum work for, rather than against you.

It rained, demanding more concentration on my part because the raindrop splashes tended to mask the surface disturbances caused by underwater rocks. A river runner must be prepared for such situations and for all weather conditions. Barbara and I can remember running a river in a snowstorm.

During a break in the rain we stopped for lunch. We were an odd-looking crew. Cisco was the most bizarre with his big black hat, yellow slicker, red life jacket, and bare legs. Mardi had taken the opposite approach, wearing oversized bright blue waterproof overalls, but with bare arms and shoulders. To my knowledge, no one has yet come up with river-chic.

We passed Loon Creek and stopped a short distance beyond on the right. The campsite was close to the river. There was a sandy strip just back from a row of ponderosa pines. We pitched tents and set up the kitchen area. A strong wind blew upstream, and we wondered if we were going to have more rain. Fortunately, the rain held off.

Next day we had only a few miles to go on the river, so we

decided not to leave until after lunch. Eric and Jayne wanted to hike up to a higher altitude, looking for some small lakes. Others wanted to fish or bathe in the hot spring that was a short way up the Loon Creek trail. Frank Allison's cabin had been burned down so I wasn't interested in hiking up the trail. Barbara and I stayed in camp, as did Mark, and also Del, who was not feeling well.

The opposite bank looked familiar, a steep bank and then a shelf before the rise of the canyonside. I suspected that this shelf was the site of the 1942 plane wreck. Mark and I crossed the river in his raft. We climbed the bank and walked upstream on the flat, between large rocks protruding from the grass and through an open stand of ponderosas. I suspected that this bench was the remains of an old landslide like the one at Sulfur Slide, only on a larger scale. Perhaps most of the material was swept down Loon Creek and blocked the river. If so, there must have been a ferocious rapid at this spot, maybe hundreds of years ago, but now the river flowing past the cut bank was quite tame.

The bench was higher than I remembered, but I saw that it was lower to the south, upstream. We followed a faint trail that wound between the rocks and wild rose bushes. We ate the rose hips, Mark commenting on their high vitamin C content. Then the bench dipped to a lower level and there were fewer trees. The place looked very familiar.

About twenty yards ahead I saw something lying on the ground between two large rocks. "Here it is," I said, and hurried ahead. We found two wooden struts embedded in the soil with grass growing up around them. The pieces were flat, pointed at both ends, made of straight-grained cedar. There were metal hinges and linkage pieces attached to the wood. On the underside of one piece, protected from the weather, we found orange fabric. We also found bits of red and silver fabric, bits of broken glass, both clear and blue, and a small piece of sheet aluminum. I looked toward the river and saw that the wreck would have been easily visible as I had floated by. Across the river, the wind sock of the Loon Creek landing strip hung limp in the still air. I said to Mark, "Look, we're right at the end of the strip. The plane lost power on take-off and spun in."

Back at camp, I fished for a while, catching and releasing a few ten-inch cutthroat that were resting in the eddies behind rocks. A kayaker came by, and we talked.

"Where are the big waves?" he asked.

"Perhaps you'll find some down in the Impassable Canyon," I answered, "but the water is pretty low."

He was off with the current, and I went back to the campground.

Del, who has a degree in anthropology, had found flakes of chert in the sandy area near the ponderosa pines. He had also found a small tool. I suggested that the Indians might have used its sharp edge and hooklike point to slit open trout, but Del said it takes a real expert with a microscope to determine how a tool was used. Still, I liked my trout-cleaning hypothesis. I took stock of the area and decided that there was a lot to eat here in addition to trout in the river and deer in the hills. Where the hill started to climb in back of the space where we'd camped there grew black hawthorn, black chokecherry, wild rose, and serviceberry. Barbara and I had brought the usual field guides on this trip, and our tree book said that all of these plants produce edible fruit. I wondered if this had been the site of a regular Indian encampment.

The other members of our group drifted back into camp. Eric and Jayne never found their lakes. Cisco had a good soak in the hot spring. Mardi and Dottie went for a hike and saw a rattlesnake. Rene caught a big cutthroat trout and dutifully released it. We ate lunch, loaded the rafts, and were off.

There was some fine scenery on this day's short run, scenery I didn't remember because in 1942 I had paddled here at full speed, my eyes on the river, covering in one day the distance that in 1982 we covered in three. We passed by craggy places on the canyon walls. The cliffs were of different-colored rock and some had yellow lichen growing on them. This was a dry area, with vegetation more sparse than farther upstream, but there was a scattering of ponderosa pine and Jeffrey fir. The river was mostly fast but with some big pools. As we drifted through one pool, we looked down through the clear water and saw twenty-inch trout swimming far below. We approached the end of the pool and were caught by an accelerating current. The rocky bottom rushed up to meet us. A few wrinkles appeared on the surface, but the water was still as clear as glass. Then we dropped over the lip onto the turbulent and noisy incline. The bottom was masked by the broken surface.

We swept around a corner and came to Hospital Bar, so named because ranchers pastured their sick cattle and horses here. Del pointed out a cascade of water pouring from a rock and falling into a natural pool right beside the river. A hot spring. We drifted by and landed a hundred yards downstream. It was a delightful spot, a large, flat area in a grove of ponderosa with the river circling around it. Barbara and I pitched our tent, put on our bathing suits, and walked upstream for a soak in the hot spring. Then Barbara did some fishing. She had a new line for her fly rod, and her casts were perfect, the line shooting out straight over the river, the fly dropping gently on the surface, but no trout rose to the challenge.

In the morning we made our usual slow start. Mardi and Dottie went upstream to skinny-dip in the hot spring. While they were in the pool, down the river came a flotilla of sweep-rafts. This was Mac Thompson's navy, a Forest Service inspection trip carrying Forest Service VIPs and members of the Idaho Water Resources Commission. One raft came close to the hot spring and a stern voice called out, "You girls will have to put on your clothes or I'll ticket you."

Dottie, who somewhat resembles a young Marilyn Monroe,

lifted a foot out of the pool, reached for a sock and slipped it on. "Certainly, officer," she said.

When Dottie and Mardi, no longer in the buff, came back to camp and told their story, we all had a good laugh. It seems strange that the Forest Service can ticket a person for being without clothes but not for being without a life jacket, but on balance, they're no more confused in their priorities than anyone else.

On this day we came to Tappan Falls. We landed on the right and had lunch while we studied the drop, which Del, Cisco, Mark, and Eric treated with considerable respect. I easily identified my old route, on the far side of a big rock two-thirds of the way across the river, definitely not a possibility at this low stage of water. We stuck with the main current on the right, though each raft took a slightly different course. It was a good drop; Cisco put it at six feet, Del said four, so my memory of five feet was about right.

When we reached Sheep Creek, our assigned campground, we found another group occupying our space. They had a legitimate reason for being there. They had been delayed on the river because they had helped in the rescue of a woman, not a member of their group, who had broken her leg in a fall on the riverbank. Using their folding table as a stretcher, they had carried the woman to the Loon Creek airstrip. The mail plane had just flown in and been able to take the woman to a hospital. The table went along with the victim, so there was a delay until the plane could bring it back. The party had had no chance of reaching their assigned campground. Sheep Creek was empty, so they had stopped there. The leader of the group apologized, but there was no problem as there was adequate space for us to camp upstream.

I found it an interesting coincidence that the woman was a passenger in a Helfrich boat. Prince Helfrich was Woodie Hindman's partner and was probably with Hindman, one day ahead of me, in 1942. The rescuing party was a Hatch group, led by Barry Hatch, grandson of Bus Hatch, who was one of the leaders of the 1936 Middle Fork expedition. Both families, Hatches from Utah and Helfriches from Oregon, have been operating on the river for years.

While we were finishing supper, a good lasagne cooked in a Dutch oven, we were joined by Barry Hatch and one of his boatmen. We had a party that lasted late into the evening. Mardi and the boatman found they had a mutual friend. Barry and Cisco talked about the problems of operating a rafting company. (Cisco has his own company in New Mexico, where he has a franchise to take paying passengers down the Box of the Rio Grande.) Barry commented that he would rather take a party of people who don't know each other on a river trip than a family group or a group of business associates. With the family or business group, all sorts of buried tensions can come boiling to the surface after a few days on the river. The boatman said that he considers himself more of an expert at dealing with problem passengers than in handling rapids. Barry and Del discussed the various U.S. agencies that regulate whitewater river use. Both gave high marks to the Forest Service. Barry and I talked about his father, with whom I've corresponded, and his grandfather. Barbara and I, with our sons Kin and Del, took a Hatch raft trip on the Green River through Dinosaur National Monument in 1959. Bus Hatch drove us to the put-in place; we had a long talk about whitewater rivers, principally about the Middle Fork. Bus is no longer running rivers in the land of the living.

Next day we floated past the old Crandall Ranch, now a guest ranch called the Flying B because of its airstrip. Up on the high bank we saw a long string of vacationers on horseback. They watched us and we watched them. Then Del took us through Haystack Rapid, and I had the strange sensation of floating between rocks that I had floated over in 1942. The wrinkled elephant-nose rock and the lizard rock were still there, though the lizard rock was beginning to split in two. In another forty years the division may be complete.

This was the end of the middle section of the river. Now the canyon grew narrower and higher, and the rapids grew steeper and more turbulent so that Del was kept busy at the oars. We passed a herd of bighorn sheep, the ewes on a sloping meadow above a cliff, and two rams at water's edge. We drifted on, in an ever-narrowing canyon. When we reached Big Creek, I saw that the suspension bridge was gone and that it had been replaced by a truss bridge, not nearly so elegant. Just below Big Creek, we stopped for the night at Last Chance Camp. Those of us who had fishing licenses hiked up Big Creek and caught fish for dinner.

Next morning we headed into the Impassable Canyon. In the six preceding days my memory had been jogged by individual rapids or sections of canyon, but now every twist and drop of the river and every configuration of the canyon wall seemed familiar. Here I had seen two eagles; there were the ledges where I had seen a primitive ladder; there was the great rock on which had been perched a log, left by some previous flood. The rock was still there, but the log was gone, carried away by some greater flood in the intervening years. We passed by Veil Falls, in front of its giant cave. I was now on the lookout for Redside Rapid. When we reached it, Del pulled over to the left bank. Cisco, Mark, and Eric followed. Just as I remembered, the water dropped among large boulders, though I was unable to identify my sneak route on the far right. Perhaps I could have spotted it if the water had been higher, or perhaps rocks had rolled into the river, adding to the rapid, or perhaps some had been washed away. We scouted the rapid carefully and then ran it, one raft at a time.

Next was Weber. We landed well upstream of the main drop and on the right. Del, Mark, Cisco, and Eric went downstream and climbed out onto a large rock that protruded into the river. I realized that this rock was the one that I had been passing close by when I flipped over in my kayak, only then the water line was right at the top of the rock while now the rock stood six or more feet above the water line.

We were about to start when two rafts came downriver and stopped near us. A young man and a young woman were in each raft. One of the oarsmen took a quick look downstream and said, "Well, it's obvious there's only one place to run this rapid." From this viewpoint, the rapid didn't look at all obvious to me, and it was made more complex by the low water. Our four rafts went through in sequence, all managing quite well, but the young man who didn't bother to scout hung up on a rock. When he broke loose and finished the run, he passed close by and said to Del, "You ran it so easily I thought I'd add some excitement."

Weber has a history of catching the unwary and the overconfident. Our group had done relatively little scouting from the bank, but I thought that the choices of where to scout and where to rely on a quick look downstream had been reasonable. We also had recourse to several guidebooks, the reputations of the various rapids, plus the memory of previous runs by Del, Cisco, Eric, and myself. Our choices had not been conservative but neither had they been based on macho impulse.

We drifted down a short distance and stopped for lunch. I walked downstream and located the spot where I had come ashore after my upset, riding the bottom of my overturned boat. I looked for the cairn that I had built, but I couldn't find it. It had either been knocked down by slide-rock or washed away by an exceptionally high flood.

After lunch we drifted through more rapids, none very difficult, to our campsite for our last night on the river. Few parties camped here because there was very little level ground to sleep on and there was no privy. We were stopping because this was Nugget Creek, where I had spent my last night in the canyon in 1942. We fitted our small tent into a sandy place between rocks and then I showed Barbara the cabin where I had taken refuge from the rockfall. Nothing much had changed, the three big ponderosas, the rocky beach; everything looked the same. Mark hiked up the canyonside, following Parrott's old trail and even finding some of his ladders. When Mark came back, he reported that he had found the remains of Parrott's upper cabin, and even three peach trees, in bad need of pruning. There were meadows up there, and Mark had seen elk and deer.

We finished supper sitting on rocks and huddled close to our small campfire. I told the others that when I was here before, also eating my supper late at night, the quiet of the canyon was shattered by the noise of rocks falling from the cliffs and possibly by the noise of gunfire. I had brought along a fifth of Canadian whiskey, and we drank a toast to the shade of the eccentric hermit who lived here and even when alive seemed to haunt the canyon. Then Cisco broke out his harmonica and over the glowing coals of the campfire played a mournful "Red River Valley." The moon rose over the canyon wall. At length, Barbara and I found our way to our tent and turned in.

In the morning, half of our group climbed up to Parrott's upper cabin. Barbara and I stayed down below. We gave the lower cabin a closer examination. The poles that had formed the bunk were gone, and there were more holes in the roof, but the cabin was essentially unchanged. The structure was simple and efficient. Parrott did a good job both in design and construction. Some shingles had been nailed to the sides and roof of the cabin. I suspected that they were the same shingles that I had found still bundled beside the cabin. If so, then Parrott made repairs to the cabin after my stopover. We heard voices from above us on the canyon wall. We looked up and saw Cisco, Mark, and Eric on their way down. They were about a hundred and fifty feet up. I called to ask them to throw stones into the river, which they did easily, but the splashes made by the stones hitting the water were unimpressive. I remembered tall columns of water rising out of the river, close to the center, not on the near side. So whether it was Parrott who bombarded me or an accident of nature, I will never know for sure.

We loaded our rafts for the last time and headed downstream. There were a number of big rapids to be run, and as we went through them, I tried to relate them to my previous run. Cliffside was more of a hazard because the gravel bar I had floated over was now high and dry; we were forced closer to the undercut cliff. Rubber was a sudden sharp drop through a narrow gap but without much of an outrun, certainly not the great beast of a rapid that I remembered. Hancock was more interesting, some rock dodging at the top, a big rock blocking the view downstream, a swing to the right and then a swing to the left through the final drop. Beyond that were some of the best rapids of the trip. The river was quite narrow, and the current swirled between rocks that jutted out of the water far enough to block any downstream view. Del was enjoying exploring these labyrinths. We hit one rock. Barbara and I moved quickly to the downstream tube of the raft, countering the force of the water which tended to make the raft climb the rock and present its vulnerable upper surface to the force of the current. In this case, Del got us off quickly.

We stopped for lunch where a ledge sloped down into a deep pool. As we were all climbing ashore, Dottie fell backward among boulders. Pain showed on her face. Barbara helped her up and comforted her. Mardi spread the plastic sheet and put out the last of the crackers, cheese, sardines, and other lunch food. The beer was long since gone, but we had filled our canteens from side creeks.

Rene walked upstream with his spinning rod. Barbara set up her fly rod. I dug into my fly box and gave her a fan-wing royal coachman. On her first cast the fly fluttered down to the surface and was met by a cutthroat torpedoing up from the depths of the pool. The fish made repeated underwater runs, pulling out line, but Barbara brought it in, a fifteen-inch trout, which she then released. Cisco exclaimed, "Man, can that lady fish!"

We realized that we hadn't seen another boating party since the two couples on their rafts had passed us below Weber. We were achieving the kind of isolation that makes it possible to enjoy a river trip to the utmost. We didn't know whether it was just chance or whether the Forest Service's system of spreading out parties along the river was beginning to work.

"Where is everybody?" Cisco asked.

"Maybe they know something we don't know," Mark suggested. "Perhaps the rest of the world has been destroyed, and we're all that's left."

"If that's the case, then you young people know your responsibility," I told them.

Laughter. But joking aside, the feeling of detachment, the feeling that the rest of the world has disappeared, not in a big bang, but by magic, and that this canyon, this river, these few people, or even this one person constitutes the only reality, is the core of the wilderness experience. The term "wilderness experience" evokes a variety of images: John Muir studying the remnants of glaciers in the High Sierra; Thoreau fishing the East Branch of the Penobscot; the prophet Elijah fed by ravens; a young Indian solemnly starting out on his vision quest; Jesus remaining forty days in the wilderness and then returning to Galilee "with the power of the spirit in him." These and many more. They share the common element of placing at a distance the pervasive ethic that requires that all thought, all values, all people, all creatures, all features of earth be subject to design and manipulation. That ethic is insatiable and seems like a demented, howling beast that seeks to destroy any corner of earth that has escaped it.

So far, this canyon had escaped. The ten of us had distanced ourselves from that destructive face of the world. For me, this forty-year-later run of the river hadn't had the intensity of my first encounter. It had not been so much a rite of passage, a loss of innocence, but I had, once again, experienced the river as healer and teacher. I sensed that Barbara, Del, Mardi, Dottie, Rene, Cisco, Mark, Eric, and Jayne had all gained from this canyon voyage. I suspect that everyone who floats these rapids and views these rock walls shares some common cleansing of the soul and is the better for it.

We picked up the remains of our lunch, folded the plastic

sheet, stowed everything in the rafts, and shoved off. Del guided us through the last twists of the canyon and down the remaining rapids.

During the eight days that we had drifted downriver, I had anticipated certain rapids, certain scenes with a particular intensity of feeling, because of some risk survived or some strong impression received on my first voyage. Invariably, when I reached the spot, I found that my memory was true, and invariably the encounter conjured up something of my original feelings. There remained one final scene. We slipped through Goat Creek Rapid, turned a corner, and looked down the mile-long and final dark corridor of the Middle Fork to where the canyon opened, almost like a door, to the brightly lit canyon of the Main Salmon. This was where, forty years earlier, I could actually see the end point and where anxiety had slipped from me like water from the deck of my boat. Viewed once more, the scene brought back the original feeling.

We eased down the final mile, then out onto the broad and swift Main Salmon. After two miles, Del pulled us over to the right bank and grounded us gently on a concrete ramp that sloped up out of the water to a parking lot where our vehicles were waiting. With very little conversation, we unloaded the rafts and carried all the duffle ashore. Then we detached the rowing frames, sloshed water into the rafts, and tipping them over, flushed out every bit of sand and gravel that might have become wedged between the big tubes and the floor. We hauled the rafts up the ramp, opened valves, and squeezed out air—these and many other tasks. A river trip is an exercise in detail.

A river trip is also an exercise of the spirit. The psyche, as well as the equipment, demands attention. When Cisco drove his big four-by-four down onto the ramp so that we could load the rafts, he slapped a tape into his tape deck. We were suddenly bathed in music. It was swing with a country-and-western accent. Mardi handed an oar to Cisco, and then she began to dance, slapping bare feet on concrete, twirling down to the water's edge and then up the ramp again.

Mardi danced, Rene and Dottie danced, Barbara and I danced.

THE MIDDLE FORK LIVES

Photo by Mary Ann Stagner

About the author:

Born in New York and educated at Yale (in mathematics), Eliot DuBois took to whitewater while still in his teens. His somewhat unscheduled descent of the Middle Fork in 1942 was the first time the river had been run solo—one person, one boat—a feat not repeated for 10 years.

Following his Idaho experience, DuBois led trips and instructed in whitewater canoeing programs in the Boston area for a number of years. He helped introduce whitewater slalom to the U. S. in the 1950s, and won the men's single foldboat race during the National Whitewater Slalom Championships in Vermont in 1958. Long active in the Appalachian Mountain Club, DuBois was also a co-founder of the American Whitewater Affiliation.

Now a resident of Monrovia, California, DuBois has continued to publish articles on whitewater topics in outdoor and canoeing publications. DuBois comes by his writing skills naturally: his mother, before her death in 1986 at age 95, had published 41 books ranging from children's books to historical novels to detective stories.

Other books from The Mountaineers include:

KEEP IT MOVING: Baja by Canoe, by Valerie Fons
Gripping narrative of a 2411-mile canoe adventure around the Baja California peninsula, where a veteran paddler and a beginner learn to be a team.

WASHINGTON WHITEWATER, 2: A Guide to 17 of Washington's Expert Whitewater Trips, by Douglass North
Detailed guidebook, loaded with photos, maps, logs and water curves, for river stretches to challenge intermediate, advanced and expert kayakers and rafters.

THE LAKES OF YELLOWSTONE: A Guide for Hiking, Fishing & Exploring, by Steve Pierce
Full descriptions and access directions for 49 lakes accessible by car or day-hike; plus capsule information on another 49, some of which require longer hikes or backpacking. Includes full information on which lakes have fish, and what kinds.

GLACIER BAY NATIONAL PARK: A Backcountry Guide to the Glaciers & Beyond, by Jim DuFresne
Complete introduction to this fabulous wilderness park, plus full details on all areas reachable only by kayak as well as those accessible by foot, tour ship or float plane. A guide for hikers, boaters and tourists.

CANOE ROUTES: Northwest Oregon, by Philip N. Jones
Details, maps and photos for 50 one-day flatwater trips in the Lower Columbia River and Willamette valley, and along the north ocean coast. For all skill levels.

For complete catalog of more than 100 outdoor titles, write:
The Mountaineers
306 Second Avenue W., Seattle WA 98119
(206) 285-2665